WORKBOOK

Keep Sharp

Build a Better Brain at Any Age

by

Sanjay Gupta M.D.

(PATIFI)

Disclaimer: Please note that this book is a companion book written to go along with the main book and should no way serve as a replacement to Sanjay Gupta's book: KEEP SHARP

This is an independent and unofficial work written in accordance to KDP's publishing guidelines for companion guides and has not been approved by the author or publisher of the main book.

TABLE OF CONTENTS

INTRODUCTION

INTRODUCTION

The brain has always been a part of the body that seemed really hard to understand as it performs a lot of functions that can be hard to explain. Our brain makes us who we are through our mind and consciousness; which is the biggest mystery of the brain. We tend to disregard the impact our lifestyle habits could have on the brain presently and in the long run, hence the need for this book.

There are many misconceptions about the brain, how it works and how to enable it function better. This book will teach you the truth about myths regarding the brain, how to live with and possible prevent Alzheimer's and other cognitive diseases, how to change your lifestyle habits in order to have a more productive brain, the process of recalling memories and how to overcome the emotional toll of caregiving.

CHAPTER 1

WHAT MAKES YOU YOU

This Chapter's Objectives

- Knowing the brain.
- Understanding the inner workings of your memory.
- The phases of memory building.

CHAPTER SUMMARY

When people are asked to imagine the brain, their visualization is always a little off. The brain is pinkish with white yellow patch instead of being gray; it contains sulcis, gyris and deep fissures that separate different aspects of the brain and it is more like gelatin instead of rubbery. Once you see the brain, you realize how vulnerable it really is despite all the things it does. Although it is usually compared to a computer; the brain does so much more. The brain doesn't have a fixed storage capacity; it actively calculates and interprets the world around us. The brain takes the inverted image we see and turns it into a 3-dimensional image providing our blind spots with data we do not even realize we processed; this is something the most advanced AI cannot accomplish. Compared to other animals, humans have a large brain and our ability to think is what sets us apart. We have the ability to eat, sleep, reproduce and survive like other animals but we also perform advanced tasks thanks to our cerebral cortex. The brain has a larger surface area than you think because it folds on itself and between these folds lays the seat of consciousness. The human brain has 100 billion neurons that are linked by synapses which helps us think, feel, make decisions, explore creativity, remember events, communicate, smell, see, experience emotions etc. Different parts of the brain have different purposes and they all work together to function in a harmonized manner.

In the olden days, the brain was thought to be divided by purpose; a part for abstract thoughts, a part for grey areas of situations; a part for language etc. but it was the incident of Phineas Gage that helped scientists get a true understanding of how the brain works. In 1848 a long rod shot up into his face through his left cheek all the way out of his head. His left eye got blinded and even though he didn't die, doctors were really able to discover how trauma to certain parts of the brain can affect a person's behavior and personality. Phineas Gage experienced a lot of seizures in his lifetime and he was one of neuroscience's famous patients. Towards the end of his life it was noted that he became less aggressive and more calming showing scientists that the brain can heal itself by a process called Neuroplasticity. Neuroplasticity is the brain's ability to once again establish the connections and networks that was damaged during trauma. This shows us the ability of the brain to change and be dynamic. After Phineas Gage, it took another century for scientists to realize that the unique abilities of the brain are not due to anatomical divisions. Our complex responses and behaviors are made up of the circuitry and communication between the various parts of our brain. Many parts of the brain develop at different rates and stages throughout our lives which is why adults solve problems faster and differently than children. When most people think about the brain, they think about the part that gives them their identity. They think about the mind which holds consciousness expressed in form of our inner voice which directs thoughts, emotions and decisions. Moments of jealousy, rage, fear etc. also comes from the brain as it takes in information and translates into these emotions.

We cannot precisely state if the mind is the brain or a part of the brain. It is easy to tell you how the brain aids functions such as walking, sight etc. but there is no exact explanation for the presence of your awareness and consciousness. To get to the brain the skin is cut first, then the skull before you sight the brain. The brain has no sensory receptors which is why surgery can be performed when a person is awake. The brain floats in a clear liquid and has no known smell. If too much pressure is placed on a part of the brain, a person could lose certain function which is why some brain surgeries are performed while the patient is awake. It is probably because the brain is located in the skull that is treated as a black box and viewed in terms of how it receives and translates information. The brain is an irreplaceable part of the body unlike some other organs and although so many researchers have studied it, no one can pinpoint what exactly makes it function or stops its function. This is why some neurodegenerative diseases are hard to understand. We might never be able to fully understand how the brain works and that is okay. Maybe we aren't supposed to know how our mind works. The brain is more than just what it does; it is what makes you human and uniquely you.

BRAINY FACTS

1. The average human brain weighs 2-2.5% of the body's overall weight and yet it consumes 20% of the body's entire energy and oxygen.
2. The brain is about 73% water so it takes 2% dehydration to damage your attention, memory and other cognitive skills. It can be restored by drinking a few ounces of water.
3. The brain is somewhat more than 3 pounds in weight. The brain's fat accounts for 60% of its dry weight making it the fattiest organ in the body.
4. Brain cells are not the same. There are different types of neurons, each with a distinct purpose.
5. The brain is the last organ in the body to reach full maturity. The human brain doesn't reach full development till a person is 25 years.
6. Brain information may travel at speeds of up to 250 miles per hour which is faster than some race cars.
7. A low-wattage LED light can be powered by the electricity generated by your brain.
8. The average person's brain is expected to generate tens of thousands of thoughts per day.
9. The brain receives 750-1000 milliliters of blood every minute. This is more than enough to fill a wine bottle.
10. A visual image can be processed in less time than it takes you to blink.
11. When compared to the average individual, the hippocampus, the memory region of the brain, has been demonstrated to be much larger in people with high cognitive demands.
12. Your brain begins to slow down around the age of 24, just before reaching full maturity at 25, but it peaks at different times for different cognitive talents.

THE ESSENCE OF MEMORY, THINKING AND HIGH MENTAL FUNCTIONING

Memory can be regarded as the mother of all wisdom and everything about us. What you see, smell or hear are memories that form your experiences in life giving a sense of identity. Memories give us the feeling of being alive, capable and valuable. They also make us feel at ease with certain people and in certain spaces. They connect your past with the present and provide a structure for the future. Negative memories can also be helpful in avoiding specific situations and making better decisions. Memory is the most well-known cognitive function and it is a higher brain function. Writing, reading, abstract thinking, making decisions, driving, admiring the works of people etc. are all examples of cognitive function. Memory is the foundation of all learning as it is where we store and absorb information. Our memories select what information is important, maintaining and selecting where it fits with previously stored information. What we save in our memory helps us deal with new challenges.

A lot of people mistake memory for memorizing and they are different things. We tend to see memory as a place where we store information when they are not of use but the memory is dynamic. Our memories change constantly as we take in and interpret new information. New information and experiences can change your memories and your brain's point of view. The fact that you can remember details of a previous event is not a survival skill. The memory's function is more about assisting in the construction and maintenance of a cohesive life narrative that is consistent with whom you are while simultaneously changing with new experiences. This dynamism helps to explain why our memories aren't always exact or objective records of the past. Memories can be modified quickly even for people with no memory issues. When you read an article or a newspaper, you are employing information you already have tucked away in your memory as you digest new information. This new knowledge also awakens certain established beliefs and ideas that are unique to you and help you understand and integrate it into your worldview before you decide to keep or forget the information. So when you read an article, your memory evolves by adding new information and finding a new place to store it. You are also providing yourself with a new mechanism to connect new information with older information.

Memory is a learning process and you update your memories every time you use it. When you talk about improving or preserving memory, you must first define what memory is and what it means to each individual. A lot of people are concerned with their ability to recall thinks but you should also be concerned about the memory required to excel in any function you play as a parent, sibling, friend, and professional etc. The more you know about your memory, the more motivated you'll be to make it better. Neuroscientists often described the memory like a filing cabinet that keeps a person's different memories but now we know that the memory cannot be described in such a static manner. The memory is more complicated and dynamic; it is not confined to or created in a single part of the brain. When functioning at full throttle, it is a brain-wide active collaboration that engages every portion of it. The memory relies on a large, distributed network that coordinates interactions through slow-frequency theta waves which is why neuroscientists are trying to develop a non-invasive electric currents to physically harmonize the neural circuits. Construction of a memory is about reassembling distinct memory or impressions from a pattern of cells present in the brain. Therefore, your memory is a network of systems, each of which plays a distinct role in the creation, storage and recollection of information. All these systems work together to create a thought when your brain processes information making a single memory an outcome of a complex architecture. When trying to recall a memory, your brain doesn't just grab a picture of what it looked like; it retrieves names, behaviors, sounds and your feelings towards that memory. Therefore, your comprehensive memory is gotten due to these characteristics.

Scientists studying the brain are now only beginning to grasp how the various parts come together to form a memory. Recalling a memory is similar to putting together a large jigsaw puzzle. The components come together to form an image or scenario and the puzzle grows in size, meaning and complexity till you've gathered enough information to complete the memory. Therefore, for a memory to work the right pieces must be present and come together appropriately. Improving your memory cannot just be done using tricks; you have to work on the different functions of your brain. Memory building can be considered in 3 phases; encoding, storage and retrieval.

BUILDING A MEMORY (ENCODING)

Encoding, which begins with your perception of an experience through your senses, is the first step in creating a memory. When you think about your memory of someone you love, you realize the first time you met your eyes, ears and nose registered their smell, voice and physical attributes. These sensations go to the hippocampus which integrates these impressions as they occur. While memory function is aided in various parts of the brain, the hippocampus is your brain's memory center. With the help of the frontal cortex, your hippocampus analyzes these many sensory inputs and determines whether or not they are worth remembering. You need to know how memory and learning works on a molecular level to understand why the tactics recommended later on will work. All your observations are analyzed and filtered using the brain's language of electricity and chemical messengers. An endpoint known as the synapse connects nerve calls to other cells. Electrical pulses carrying signals leap through extremely small spaces between the cells causing chemical messengers known as neurotransmitters to be released. Examples of neurotransmitters are epinephrine, dopamine etc. these neurotransmitters attach themselves to nearby cells as they migrate across the spaces between the cells. There are trillions of synapses in the average brain. Dendrites which are treelike short branched extensions of a nerve cell stretch out to the neighboring brain cells and receive these electrical impulses. The connections between brain cells are very dynamic in nature; they are constantly changing, growing and shrinking. Brain cells organize themselves into specialized groupings to function in different types of information processing as they work together in a network. The synapses between two brain cells strengthen when one transmits messages to the other. The link becomes stronger as a particular signal is delivered more frequently hence the saying "Practice makes perfect". Your brain rewires a little every time you encounter something new to accommodate that new experience.

New dendrites emerge as a result of new experiences and learning while old dendrites become more established as a result of repeated behaviors and learning. Plasticity is the formation of new dendrites, even if they are weak. This plasticity can aid in the rewiring of your brain if it is injured. It is also a key component of resilience which is necessary for brain development. As you explore the environment and learn new things, changes occur at the synapses and dendrites, with more connections being formed and others being weakened. The brain is constantly reorganizing itself in response to your experiences, education and memories and with constant use, the neural changes are strengthened. The brain generates detailed circuits of knowledge and memory as you learn mew material and practice new skills. If you do a task repeatedly, your brain makes it easier to replicate till you can perform it perfectly but if you stop practicing for a few weeks, you will not be as perfect as you were because your brain begins to forget. This is because the dendrites that were defined begin to fade away and in order to be perfect you must rebuild those neural connections.

There is a warning you should take note of when making memories. To encode a memory correctly, you must pay attention. You must be aware of what you are experiencing because you cannot pay attention to everything you see as a lot of stimuli automatically get filtered out. Only a few stimuli actually reaches your conscious consciousness because if your brain recalled everything it saw, its memory system would be overloaded to the point where basic functions would be difficult to execute. Scientists are divided on if stimuli are screened out after the brain has processed their meaning or during the sensory input stage. The way you pay attention to incoming data could be the most crucial determinant in how much information you recall eventually. Forgetting has a very important value in the brain as remembering everything would overwhelm your brain. A group of neurons are responsible for assisting the brain in forgetting and they are most active at night when the brain reorganizes itself preparing for a new intake of information. In 2019, scientists identified these forgetting neurons which aid our understanding of the necessity of sleep and the importance of forgetting. To remember, you must to some extent forget.

SHORT-TERM VERSUS LONG-TERM MEMORY (STORAGE)

Our memories are divided into 2 categories: short-term memory and long-term memory. There is however a sensory stage that lasts a fraction of a second before an experience can be part of your short-term memory. Your impression of an experience is recorded in your brain during this stage when you register incoming information such as what you see, hear and feel. Sensory memory allows that perception to persist after the stimulation has ended and the sensation is stored as short-term memory. Most people can hold about 7 items of information in their short-term memory at once and it can be increased using different tricks and strategies. You must transfer knowledge from short-term to long-term memory in order to retain and recall it. Short-term memory is tightly tied to the hippocampus function but long-term memory is closely linked to the activities of the cerebral cortex.

All of the information you can truly know and recall is stored in long-term memory; it becomes a part of you. You can access information that has been stored in your long-term memory for a very long time. Long-term memory allows us to recall functions and store a limitless quantity of data eternally. However, certain situations can cause the process of transferring a memory from short to long term be disrupted and an example is alcohol. An intoxicated person cannot encode well into their long-term memory. Sleep deprivation cannot obstruct the transition of short-term to long-term memories. Your body transfers short-term memories to long-term memories while you sleep so a lack of sleep disrupts that process.

RETRIEVAL

Without retrieval, none of this works. When you recall a memory, you initially retrieve the information on an unconscious level before consciously transferring it to your conscious mind. A lot of people who think they have excellent memory are just really good at remembering some things. If you have trouble recalling people's names when you have no physical illness or dementia, you probably weren't paying attention or you have an inefficient retrieval system. This can be remedied by sharpening your memory skills for encoding and retrieval.

Memory issues appear to worsen with age for some people. In our twenties, our memory speed and accuracy gradually begin to deteriorate especially our working memory, which temporarily stores knowledge in the mind so we can make good decisions through the day. Memory issues aren't a given as people become older; there are things a person can do to keep, improve and sharpen their memory retention and retrieval capacities as they live.

QUESTIONS / EXERCISE

What were your initial thoughts on the brain before reading this chapter?

_____

_____

_____

_____

_____

_____

_____

_____

What are the negative effects of sleep deprivation on the brain?

_____

_____

_____

_____

_____

_____

_____

_____

_____

_____

What is neuroplasticity?

_____

_____

_____

_____

_____

_____

_____

_____

What is your usual level of awareness in situations?

_____

_____

_____

_____

_____

_____

_____

_____

_____

_____

_____

_____

Personal Notes, Lessons and Action Plans

CHAPTER 2

COGNITIVE DECLINE – REDEFINED

This Chapter's Objectives

- Understanding the different ways the brain breaks.
- Differentiating the different forms of dementia.
- Focusing on your brain.

CHAPTER SUMMARY

"What caused it? How can I help?" are usually the first questions that come to a person's mind when a loved one is struggling with cognition. They see it as a malfunction instead of a tumor, blockage or other medical anomalies. The symptoms for these cognitive struggles are usually similar and it shows that we do not know and cannot know the cause of cognitive declines as multiple things are at play. There are many theories but no definite answers and it is becoming clear that this decline starts long before the symptoms emerge. This is why younger generations need to practice habits to help prevent this decline. Although there has been progress since the first discovery of Alzheimer's, researchers still have no idea about what causes or triggers it. This shows how complex humans are because what triggers cognitive decline in people is different just like cancer. However, there are strategies to reduce your risk for dementia and to understand these strategies; we must examine the current theories on what happens in the brain of someone with Alzheimer's.

The amyloid hypothesis is the leading hypothesis in recent times. Amyloid plaques or beta-amyloid plaques build up in the brain and disrupt the crucial synapses that allow brain cells to communicate. The problem with this treatment is that it is based on an idea that has mainly failed in clinical trials. The course of this disease is more complicated than any single cause and researchers also looked at if cognitive decline is as a result of normal aging or degenerative conditions affecting specific brain networks. This is why researches are focused on triggers such as injury, nutrient deficiency, being exposed to harmful chemicals etc. which can cause an inflammatory response thereby destroying the brain. Inflammation is a much known symptom in all theories about brain decline.

EIGHT (POTENTIAL) WAYS THE BRAIN BEGINS TO BREAK

Some of the factors can contribute to the problem with some having a greater impact than others on individual risk factors.

1. THE AMYLOID CASCADE HYPOTHESIS (ACH): Dr. Aloysius Alzheimer first described this peculiar disease in a 51-year-old woman who had profound memory loss, crazy behavior and physiological changes. In an autopsy of her brain, he noticed a dramatic shrinkage and abnormal deposits he called SENILE PLAQUES in a nerve in 1907. These plaques were eventually recognized as containing beta-amyloid and today these plaques with neurofibrillary tangles are the distinctive features of Alzheimer's. amyloid plaques form between nerve cells in Alzheimer's disease and tangles primarily composed of tau protein are twisted insoluble fibers seen in the brain cells. Tau protein is a microscopic part of the brain cell that is important for

its stability and survival. However, we need beta-amyloid and tau proteins in our brains as healthy versions of them are part of our brain's biology. They aid in the provision of food to brain cells and ensure that vital substances can readily travel between them. Problems occur when beta-amyloid an tau are damaged, misfolding into sticky clumps. When amyloid fibrils transform into waterproof rope-like structures with proteins that interlock (like a zip), they go rogue. These molecular zippers clog up and become difficult to open forming plaques. The formation of plaques around the brain cells according to the ACH causes Alzheimer's disease although scientist are not sure how or why. Drugs designed to eliminate beta-amyloid in the human brain haven't worked as well as scientists hoped. The concept that beta-amyloid conveys the complete story has been shattered by a string of clinical failures based on this hypothesis. Some people with plaques in their brain show no sign of cognitive deterioration. On autopsy, these patients' brains are often discovered to be packed with plaques but they died mentally intact and while this can be attributed to a condition known as Cognitive Reserve, we do not know if plaques are an effect or cause of Alzheimer's. A 'unicorn' in the Alzheimer's world is when a dementia patient's brain autopsy only reveals plaque and tangle damage. The reason is that a damaged brain rarely shows one type of damage. The disease complexity has compelled doctors to reconsider their approach to finding a solution and there probably won't be a universal cure as people are likely to suffer from a variety of dementias. Genetics can also play a role. Anomalies in the genes that code for amyloid protein such as mutations in the Amyloid Precursor

Protein (APP), presenilin 1 and 2 genes can increase beta-amyloid production and account for the early-onset Alzheimer's that affects many members of the families that carry these mutations. Scientists have been examining mutation clans around the world where the diseases runs in families and sometimes within these clans are individuals who have the genetic profile for early-onset Alzheimer's but are somehow saved due to other unusual mutations. Scientists seek to create new medication or gene therapies by better understanding the natural history of the disease, which has significant genetic roots especially for those that do not carry Alzheimer's-causing genes but end up developing dementia.

While heredity is more likely to impact early-onset Alzheimer's disease, genes may also have a later role. The body's repair machinery for correcting DNA mutations grow less efficient as we age making it vulnerable. The dry molecular amyloid zipper described earlier could start with a single twist in the chain of amino acids but as we grow, these twists build up and the repair enzymes are no longer in control. Scientists want to understand these zippers to understand what causes Alzheimer's disease.

2. TAU AND TANGLES: Neurofibrillary tangles (NFT) are a sign of tau protein issue. Inside brain cells, tau proteins are linked to railroad tracks and they are in charge of stabilizing nerve cells in the brain and assisting communication across different parts of the brain. While they undergo chemical changes, they lose their ability to keep nerve cells together. They become tangled making them a problem instead. Because the clumping and spread of chemically altered tau protein

molecules differ from amyloid plaques, researchers are still looking for a theory that encompasses problems with tau protein as well as amyloid. The trigger and bullet paradigm where amyloid is the trigger and tau is the bullet has been mentioned in recent articles. 2/sTau proteins are also implicated in Chronic Traumatic Encelopathy (CTE) which is a degenerative brain disease linked to repetitive hits to the head and associated with behavioral issues, depression, memory loss and dementia. CTE is often seen in athletes playing high contact sports.

Prions are increasingly being mentioned in connection with plaques and tangles. Prions are a type of protein found in the brain that can cause other proteins to fold improperly. A few disorders related to prions are connected with infections and are universally fatal. The most frequent from of prion disease in humans Creutzfeldt-Jakob disease (also known as Mad Cow Disease) is from infected beef products. Some scientists are investigating if prion-like forms of amyloid and tau spread throughout the brain causing normal proteins to become misfolded and twisted triggering Alzheimer's.

3. BLOOD FLOW: People with advanced vascular disease are known to have plaques and tangles more frequently and severely. This shows that changes in brain blood flow may play a role in the progression of Alzheimer's disease. Reduced blood flow to the brain has been thought to be a pioneer to the formation of plaques and tangles. Changes in blood flow to the brain are likely to cause a crisis among neurons and their support staff cells called Gilia resulting in cell death and cognitive impairment. The brain is a highly

vascular organ that places a high demand on the circulatory system to deliver nutrients and oxygen on a continuous basis. Any factor that affects the blood flow system in the brain has a substantial impact on its function. The vascular hypothesis of Alzheimer's disease could explain why people with a history of high blood pressure or have stroke are more susceptible to the disease. High blood pressure can induce microscopic damage to the arteries leading to the brain which can limit blood flow and oxygenation. Brain cells require glucose and oxygen for energy. A problem starts when the delivery of energy to the brain is hindered by a lack of blood flow. Recent studies show that when the blood-brain barrier breaks down, blood flow to the brain is reduced. Because the brain is so valuable, it is shielded from the body's blood supply by the skull, a bath of cerebrospinal fluid and the blood-brain barrier. When functioning properly, this barrier allows oxygen, glucose and other essential substances to pass through while simultaneously preventing harmful molecules from entering the brain. As a result, the brain swells gradually, increasing the pressure inside the cranium and obstructing blood flow to the brain. The crisis in neurons and glia are reignited as a result of less oxygenated blood reaching the brain causing greater edema, lesions, production of beta-amyloid plaques and tau tangles in the brain. According to recent research, the hippocampus is particularly prone to the leaky blood-brain barrier syndrome and as the protective barrier breaks down, harmful compounds from the blood vessels can reach the neurons worsening memory loss and cognitive impairment.

4. METABOLIC DISORDERS: The large group of metabolic diseases is another major risk factor for dementia. Nearly 35% of all U.S. adults and 50% of those of 60 years or older are estimated to have metabolic syndrome. Researchers have been finding links between diabetes and Alzheimer's disease risk since 2005, especially in elderly people. Some researchers have gone as far as referring to Alzheimer's as 'type 3 diabetes' because it involves a twisted relationship with insulin which is involved in type 1 and type 2 diabetes. Insulin is a hormone that allows glucose to enter cells and be used. Cells cannot absorb glucose if they do not have insulin. A person with type 1 diabetes is unable to produce insulin because the body has destroyed the specialized cells in the pancreas required for its production and so they have to inject themselves with insulin. Type 2 diabetes is characterized by chronically high blood sugar levels that result in severe insulin spikes that cause cells to become insensitive to the hormone. The cells shutdown the receptors that bind insulin and transport it in the presence of too much insulin. A person with type 2 diabetes can generate insulin but their cells do not utilize it as well as it should causing sugar to accumulate in the bloodstream. Type 1 diabetes is caused by a malfunctioning system while type 2 diabetes is mostly caused by a poor diet. Science reveals that Alzheimer's could be as a result of a sugary Western diet.

People with type 2 diabetes are at least twice as likely to acquire Alzheimer's and people with metabolic syndrome are at a higher risk of developing predementia or mild cognitive impairment (MCI). Although not all studies support the link, evidence seems to be increasing causing scientists to reconsider their assumptions. The road from a poor diet to Alzheimer's doesn't have to be through type 2 diabetes which is why studies now show that those with high blood sugar have a faster rate of cognitive loss than people with normal blood sugar. Basically, the higher the blood sugar, the faster the decline. At the heart of type 3 diabetes is the inability of neurons in the brain to respond to insulin resulting in cell starvation and death as insulin signaling is disturbed. Insulin shortage according to some studies is crucial to Alzheimer's disease cognitive loss and may be involved in the creation of plaques. A study led by Dr. Guojun Bu, a Mayo Clinic neuroscientist and professor of medicine, provided more evidence for type 3 diabetes when he discovered that the Alzheimer's gene mutation APOE4 is responsible for disrupting how the brain processes insulin. APOE4 is prevalent in about 20% of the generational population and more than half of Alzheimer's patients. In his study, the mice with the APOE4 gene demonstrated insulin deficiency especially as they got older. When all of this data is combined, it supports the theory that heredity, bad diet and the risk of cognitive decline are linked. Not only has there been a parallel rise in the number of type 2 diabetes cases and number of obese people but there is also a record of the same pattern among people with dementia. As the prevalence of type 2 diabetes rises, so does the rate of Alzheimer's disease.

There is usually a link between weight and diabetes risk. If metabolic abnormalities increase the chance of Alzheimer's, it stands to reason that unhealthy weight gain with metabolic repercussions would also increase the risk and this is supported by science. The brain has been proven to be particularly harmed by carrying additional weight around the abdomen.

5. TOXIC SUBSTANCES: More research needs to be done to understand the chemicals that can result in brain anomalies and not well-known neurotoxins like lead but exposure to chemicals we encounter daily that could slowly cause harm. Aluminum was once thought to be a cause of Alzheimer's disease prompting many individuals to discard their pots and pans. Although aluminum's neurotoxicity is undeniable, establishing a link between aluminum and Alzheimer's is more difficult. The hypothesis that aluminum causes dementia has been debunked but there are other neurotoxins to be concerned about. In Jackson Hole, Wyoming, ethnobotanist Paul Alan Cox explores how the indigenous people interact with their environment especially plants. His research led him to Guam, where he researched the Chamorro people who were known to be 100 times more prone than the rest of the world to acquire a complex of neurological disorders including Alzheimer's. He put his skills to work and formed a collaboration of scientists from several fields to examine and what they found could eventually be useful to everyone. The Chamorro have been accidentally poisoning themselves with BMAA, a neurotoxin produced by blue-green algae, as a result of their diet. Because of this diet, they take it in high doses but it turns out that we are all exposed to BMAA which could be a significant risk factor for Alzheimer's. Proteins like amyloid and tau misfold and cluster together in plaques and tangles as a result of BMAA neurotoxicity. Therefore, Cox and some other

scientists believe that amyloid and tau are not the cause of Alzheimer's but a consequence of it. Cox's team's ongoing work into how to cure Alzheimer's disease in an easy approach is very important. They demonstrated that the misfolding of amyloid and tau doesn't proceed when one of these protein's building blocks is replaced with the amino acid L-serine, preventing the course of Alzheimer's. His team has only shown this in fervent monkeys but human studies are currently underway. The best aspect is that L-serine is readily available, has few adverse effects and is cheap.

6. INFECTIONS: It has been known that infections from various pathogens can have neurological effects. A theory is forming among experts that the body's reaction to infections can cause catastrophic forms of neurodegenerative decline. This is a controversial issue as no one knows if the presence of germs causes or accelerates the disease or if it is just a result of the disease. A study from Harvard researchers led by the late Dr. Robert D. Moir in 2016 argued that infections including mild ones that hardly elicit symptoms fire up the immune system in the brain and leave a refuse trail which is the distinctive feature of Alzheimer's. the assumption is that a virus, bacteria or fungus gets through the blood-brain barrier and activates the brain's self-defense system. To fight the invader, the brain produces beta-amyloid which acts as a sticky web that traps the invader and what is left is the webby plaque that is seen in the brain of Alzheimer patients. More research is needed in this area as not everyone who had a brain infection develops Alzheimer's and not everyone who develops dementia can be attributed to only the infection.

DR. RUDY TANZI'S "ALZHEIMER'S IN A DISH"

Dr. Rudolph Tanzi is discovered the Alzheimer's genes in the 1980s and 1990s. He also clarified the connection between some infections and Alzheimer's and since 2014, scientists have made progress in understanding the pathology of Alzheimer's thanks to his "Alzheimer's in a dish" which was the first petri-dish model of the disease. He and his colleagues generated mini-human brain organoid in a petri-dish, introduced the Alzheimer's genes and monitored what happened. He saw the plaques and tangles interact, followed by neuroinflammation and nerve cell death. Tanzi believes the brain's immune system sends a flood of inflammatory cells to put out the brushfires. The neuroinflammation then kills up to a 100 times more nerve cells paving way for dementia later on. This sequence of events according to him explains why clinical trials failed in the past. It is because they try to strike the amyloid way too late. The aim is to prevent the amyloid from forming and identify patients before the symptoms appear. According to his lab, amyloid forms almost immediately around viruses like bacteria or herpes and fungi like yeast and within 24 hours a plaque forms containing the virus. These are extracellular traps which are an important feature of our immune system. When we receive an illness, antibodies take long to kick in but our basic immune system tries to help us in the mean time. While the immune system protects us from infection, it also paves the way for Alzheimer's later in life. This isn't to say that you need germs to produce a plaque. Other ingredients can also trigger plaque formation and genetics plays a part in making some people more likely to develop plaques. This doesn't mean that some viruses aren't linked to Alzheimer's. We must note that as we get older our viral and bacterial loads from a lifetime of exposures are much higher than when we were younger. Some germs like herpes simplex virus 1 can reactivate later in life and when that happens amyloid is planted in a manner similar to cloud seeding. In order to protect the nerve cells in the brain, a large mass develops around the virus and traps it. According to Tanzi, we all need a bit of beta-amyloid to protect the brain but at some point it could be a problem. When answering why some people have a lot of brain plaques but do not have dementia, Tanzi refers to them as resilient brains. The objective is to ensure that the immune system of the brain does not overreact to neuroinflammation.

7. HEAD TRAUMA AND INJURY: Repetitive hits to the head can do lasting damage. Dr. Gary Small was the doctor who diagnosed Tony Dorsett's CTE and his group's findings was one of the first to link multiple concussions to tau buildup. Dorsett had been suffering from melancholy and memory loss and sought help at UCLA. He wanted to discover if there was a link between all of the concussions he had as a football player in the 1970s and 1980s and the severe symptoms he experienced later in his life. A lot of former football players have been diagnosed with CTE since Dorsett's diagnosis and lawsuits have been brought against the National Football League.

8. IMMUNE SYSTEM CHALLENGES AND CHRONIC INFLAMMATION: Chronic inflammation associated with aging lies at the heart of almost all degenerative disorders from those that raise dementia risk to those

that are directly brain related. Scientists have disputed the role of inflammation in a damaged brain for decades but new data reveals that inflammation not only aggravates but initiates disease processes in the brain causing a decline. Inflammation is the body's defense strategy for dealing with possible insults and injury but it becomes troublesome when that system is constantly deploying chemical compounds and activating the immune system. Previous research suggested that people who took common anti-inflammatory medications like Ibuprofen for two or more years have a lower risk of Alzheimer's and Parkinson's disease but clinical trials fails to show that it can prevent this and taking it has its own side effects. Other investigations have found elevated cytokine levels in the brains of people with this and other degenerative brain illnesses. Cytokines are chemicals generated by cells in the body that act as traffic signals for the inflammatory process. This suggests that chronic inflammation is likely to play a significant role in cognitive deterioration. New imaging technology today allows us to see cells actively implicated in the production of inflammatory cytokines in Alzheimer's patients' brains for the first time.

Inflammation in the brain can also be linked to amyloid plaques and tau tangles, demonstrating how intertwined and interlinked some of these Alzheimer's causes can be. Microglia or glia cells are specialized support staff cells in the brain that recognize these proteins as foreign waste and release inflammatory chemicals to get rid of them. Glial cells are the brain's own immune cells and they are related to macrophages which are white blood cells. The inflammation caused by the glial cells' activity further inhibits the functioning of neurons but the specific cause-and-effect is still unknown. We cannot exactly say that inflammation causes Alzheimer's disease but it is likely to play a significant role in the overall picture.

TYPES OF COGNITIVE DEFICITS

From a normal aging brain, there is no well-defined path to full-blown Alzheimer's. Alzheimer's disease is one type of dementia and each person has a unique experience. According to the Alzheimer's Association other conditions apart from Alzheimer's cause up to 40% of dementias.

NORMAL AGING

As you get older, your brain changes like the rest of your body. While there is normal age-related tissue loss and synaptic degeneration, there is a recent discovery that we should be happy about. Columbia University researchers discovered for the first time in 2018 that healthy adults can manufacture as many new brain cells as young people. The ability to generate new neurons from precursor cells in the hippocampus is not simply dependent on age according to researchers. Although older people have reduced vascularization and less ability of new neurons to form connections, they do not lose their ability to create new brain cells. It should be obvious that staying healthy is necessary to preserve neurogenesis, vascularization and the formation of new brain connections. The brain starts to age in your mid-twenties and can start to degenerate structurally as early as thirty. The hippocampus declines by around 0.5% per year after the age of 40. Individual shrinkage is varied and is greatly influenced by lifestyle choices, environment, genes and medical disorders. The hippocampus is affected by these elements more than any part of the brain. Several neuroscience investigations have found that the hippocampus is fragile and shrinks more than any other part of the brain in response to brain injuries.

We all experience a failure of the memory assembly process which starts in a moderate way when we are young and worsen as we get older. In an autopsy of an older brain, the brain has shrunk, the folds are more evident and the blood vessels have stiffened and become less durable. Under a microscope, evidence of neuronal cell death and changes in synapses may be visible. However, none of this is linked to outward signs of cognitive decline while the person was alive meaning aging doesn't mean there'll be unavoidable cognitive decline. Any cognitive decline is usually more than just a factor of age and brain degeneration.

MILD COGNITIVE IMPAIRMENT

While MCI is frequently the first stage of dementia, not everyone with MCI will progress to a more severe form of Alzheimer's disease. MCI causes a gradual, undetectable deterioration in memory. MCI affects primarily memory and it is important to address warning signs and symptoms as early as possible. MCI is believed to affect 10-20% of adults aged 65 and above.

DEMENTIA

Dementia is a general term that refers to a variety of symptoms and degrees of cognitive deterioration, ranging from mild cognitive impairment to severe dementia. It is not a single disease but a collection of underlying diseases and brain abnormalities that affect memory, communication and reasoning. It occurs in various forms;

1. Vascular Dementia: An inadequate flow of blood to the brain is the cause of this dementia. It can be caused by a blood vessel blockage or damage that leads to strokes or bleeding in the brain. Symptoms of both vascular dementia and Alzheimer's disease can appear at the same time in certain people. Dementia is determined by the location and severity of brain injury as well as how the individual's cognitive and physical functioning are affected. Evidence of vascular dementia was once used to rule out an Alzheimer's diagnosis. This is no longer done because brain changes and Alzheimer's and vascular dementia coexist. Only around 10% of dementia patients' brains show signs of only vascular dementia while about half of all Alzheimer's patients have indicators of silent strokes.

2. Dementia with Lewy Bodies (DLB): One out of every five dementia patients suffers from this. Proteins called Alpha-synuclein or Lewy bodies will accumulate in areas of the brain that control cognition, movement and behavior causing these individuals to experience memory issues and symptoms similar to Parkinson's disease. Visual hallucinations are common in the early stages of schizophrenia and can help to determine the diagnosis.

3. Frontotemporal Lobar Dementia (FTLD): It is also known as Pick's disease and is a group of disorders caused by gradual nerve cell loss in the frontal and temporal lobes of the brain causing behavioral changes. The earliest indicators are frequent changes in personality and behavior. About 60% of patients

with FTLD are between the ages of 45and 60 but FTLD accounts for only 10% of dementia cases.
4. Alzheimer's Disease: It is the most frequent type of dementia. It is an illness that progresses over time with symptoms that appear gradually befpre becoming severe. It can make it difficult for people to perform their daily duties, think rationally, control movement etc. as it progresses. Mixed dementia occurs when a person exhibits symptoms of Alzheimer's as well as other dementias.

NORMAL VERSUS NOT NORMAL

When people forget something simple they tend to ask themselves if it is normal or the beginning of cognitive decline. Mary A. Fischer stated the 6 types of normal memory failure for AARP that you shouldn't worry about and they are;

1. Absentmindedness: This happens to everyone from time to time and it can be blamed on lack of attention or focus. Harry Lorayne ad Jerry Lucas' work called The Memory Book describes the process of generating 'original awareness'. They use this term when referring to the first time you see or do something that should be remembered. Observation is needed to original awareness and it is not the same as "seeing". What the mind observes and sees are two different things. There can be no observation if you are absentminded and there can be no knowledge of the action and formation of the memory if your mind is absent when performing an action.
2. Blocking: It is a classic but annoying experience if being unable to recall something from memory that you know is right there. You know what you want to say but you can't because it is hidden. Several similar

memories cause a disruption causing blocking. It is as if your memory button gets stuck often.

3. Scrambling: This is when you are confusing minor details when you get information but you can perfectly remember most of what happened or other pieces of the information. This is most likely due to a hippocampal malfunction; it has wrongly recorded the facts.

4. Fading Away: The brain clears out old memories to make room for new ones on a regular basis. Memories that aren't recalled frequently can start to fade away since they aren't reinforced. This is why it is simpler to recall specifics from recent events. This essential use-it-or-lose-it feature of the memory is called Transcience and it occurs in all ages.

5. Struggling for Retrieval: It is similar to being absent-minded. New knowledge can remove other items from short-term memory unless it is repeated continuously as the brain ages and new information can affect the strengths of the connections between neurons in the brain. This is why you should pay attention to learning a person's name on the spot and linking it with something specific or familiar to avoid this mistake.

6. Muddled Multitasking: The amount of things you do can effectively at a time reduces at some point. According to studies, the brain requires more effort to concentrate as we become older and it takes longer to return to an initial activity after being interrupted.

RETHINKING COGNITIVE DECLINE

Because Alzheimer's disease cannot be diagnosed definitively like other diseases, it is easy to prematurely label people with it. Some people can easily reverse their cognitive decline because they never even had Alzheimer's and this is a point brought up by Dr. Majid Fotuhi who is a neurologist and neuroscientist with more than 25 years of research and clinical experience in the field of memory, aging and brain rehabilitation. He presently treats patients with a range of complex neurological issues. He claims that when he puts patients through his interdisciplinary protocols which are unique for each person, he achieves exceptional results. A comprehensive brain fitness program according to him focuses on lifestyle measures to change risk factors and in his studies he has recorded significant gains. Within weeks of an interventional program, he observed significant development in the volume of the hippocampus which is the brain's most critical memory area. He suggests we forget the terrible term Alzheimer's and use new terms like mild cognitive impairment. He also analyzed the amyloid cascade hypothesis as a basis for people with Alzheimer's. In 2009, he provided a different theory called Dynamic Polygon Theory.

He explains it in this way: Multiple risk factors and protective factors interact to help us stay sharp or quickly decline. He continues to believe that blaming amyloid as the primary cause of a decline that affects the majority of people in their later years is foolish. Amyloid is the sole cause of Alzheimer's in people with early-onset Alzheimer's which is different from the late-onset.

FOCUS ON YOUR BRAIN AND EVERYTHING ELSE WILL FOLLOW

When it comes to our health, many of us focus on weight, blood sugar, cancer risk etc. but overlook the brain. Because the brain is enclosed in the skull and has a magical nature, these other things seem easier to grasp.

The brain has traditionally been interacted with by medical personnel only when it is damaged or has a disease. Here is the thing; when you put your brain first, everything else about your health falls into place. The brain is the starting point and what defines you. You cannot make good decisions without a healthy brain and a healthy brain leads to healthy body, heart, stronger sense of confidence and so on due to wise decisions and better relationships.

QUESTIONS / EXERCISE

How often do you worry about your memory failure?

_____

_____

_____

_____

_____

_____

_____

_____

What are the potential ways to break the brain?

_____

_____

_____

_____

_____

_____

_____

What is the relationship between diabetes and Alzheimer's disease?

_____

_____

_____

_____

_____

_____

_____

How has head trauma affected your brain in the past?

_____

_____

_____

_____

_____

_____

_____

_____

_____

Personal Notes, Lessons and Action Plans

CHAPTER 3

12 DESTRUCTIVE MYTHS AND THE 5 PILLARS THAT WILL BUILD YOU

This Chapter's Objectives

- Understanding the truths behind the myths about the aging brain.
- Keeping a sharp mind.
- Understanding the concept of SuperAgers.

CHAPTER SUMMARY

When the brain survives a trauma against all odds, it is more resilient and can recover more than you think. In the worst case scenario, you can intervene to prevent the brain's final demise as you progress and learn how to change your personal circumstances to reduce your chances of experiencing a brain-related sickness or dying from one.

THE DIRTY DOZEN

There are 12 persuasive myths about the aging brain and they are known as the Dirty Dozen.

MYTH 1: THE BRAIN REMAINS A COMPLETE MYSTERY

We have a better understanding of the connections between different areas of the brain and how they affect how we think, move and feel. We can now pinpoint the brain areas responsible for depression, OCD, and addiction physically. We can also rehabilitate the brain after a stroke or injury. Neuroscience always has new breakthroughs.

MYTH 2: OLDER PEOPLE ARE DOOMED TO FORGET THINGS

There is a little truth to this myth. As you get older, some cognitive skills deteriorate especially if you do not use tactics to help you pay attention and recall. While you might have been better at learning a new language or listing things, as an adult, you're more likely to have a larger vocabulary and be a better judge of character. The other good thing about aging is that you tend to get better at managing your emotions, stress etc.

MYTH 3: DEMENTIA IS AN INEVITABLE CONSEQUENCE TO OLD AGE

Dementia is not a normal part of the aging process. Normal-aging changes in the brain are not the same as disease-related changes; you can slow down the former and avoid the latter.

MYTH 4: OLD PEOPLE CANNOT LEARN NEW THINGS

Learning can occur at any age, especially when engaging in cognitively challenging activities. We can continue to change our brain's information, capacity and learning strengths since the memory is dynamic and we can produce new neurons. Acquiring new abilities may take longer in an older person but it doesn't mean they cannot do it. Even a person with Alzheimer's can learn a new skill.

MYTH 5: YOU MUST MASTER ONE LANGUAGE BEFORE LEARNING ANOTHER

Young children study two languages and do not confuse them. Mastering two languages simultaneously might take a long time but it is possible. There is no interference as the different parts of the brain do not fight each other. Children are less self-conscious which could explain why they can easily learn a new language.

MYTH 6: A PERSON WHO HAS MEMORY TRAINING NEVER FORGETS

MYTH 7: WE USE ONLY 10% OF OUR BRAINS

This myth has existed for as long as we can remember but it is false especially from an evolutionary perspective. The brain is a demanding organ that requires a lot of energy to develop and maintain especially as an adult so it would make no sense evolutionarily to carry extra brain tissue around. Experiments with Positron-Emission Tomography (PET) scans show that even simple tasks engage a large portion of the brain and injury to small areas of the brain can have huge implications on language, movement or emotion. According to autopsy research, many people with no symptoms exhibited physical evidence of Alzheimer's in their brain. There is something to be said about using your mind at a 100%. When people are motivated, they do better in IQ tests. See the brain a s a city; important structures are used constantly and account for 10-20% of the brain. The rest are roads that connect these important structures and important information cannot reach its destination without them. Therefore, they are still required.

MYTH 8: MALE AND FEMALE BRAINS DIFFER IN WAYS THAT DICTATE LEARNING ABILITIES AND INTELLIGENCE

According to urban myths, men are biologically better suited for math and science while women are suited for empathy and intuition. Some biased research try to provide biological explanations for gender inequality. Yes, some variances occur in the brain of male and females causing difference in brain function but one are not better than the other. More research is being done to learn about differences in the male and female brain. While everyone is different we can all learn, remember etc. if we possess a healthy brain. Alzheimer's affects more females than makes. We cannot say what puts women at a higher risk but it is possible that our physiology has something to do with it.

Women have an advantage over men which could pay a role in detecting cognitive impairments. Studies show that women perform better on tests used to diagnose dementia early when compared to men. A woman's stronger language skills allow them to mask Alzheimer which prevents easy-detection and this benefit vanishes as the cognitive deterioration progresses.

MYTH 9: A CROSSWORD PUZZLE A DAY CAN KEEP THE BRAIN DOCTOR AWAY

This is another legend and unfortunately crossword puzzles only exercise a part of your brain especially its fluency but they do not exactly help to keep your entire brain sharp. However, there is an advantage in doing number puzzles such as Sudoku as it has been discovered that they help in improving abilities like reasoning and memory. The research also noted that these results do not necessarily mean that doing puzzles will improves brain function but keeping and active mind reduces thinking and some people do that using crossword puzzles.

MYTH 10: YOU ARE DOMINATED BY EITHER YOUR "RIGHT" OR "LEFT" BRAIN

The two sides of the brain are profoundly codependent on each other. People are always said to either be right-brained or left-brained. Right-brained people are believed to be more creative and artistic while left-brained people are more rational. This concept came from the observation that a lot of people express and receive language more in the left part of the brain while emotional expressions are expressed more on the right side. This concept is used a lot by psychologists to differentiate personality types. However, brain scanning technology has shown that the 2 sides of the brain work together in complex ways. Language processing is done by the 2 sides of the brain with the left side in charge of grammar and pronunciation while the right side deals with intonation.

MYTH 11: YOU HAVE ONLY FIVE SENSES

Most people can only name the known 5 senses which are sight, smell, taste, touch and hearing. However, there are 6 other senses processed in the brain giving us more information about the world and they include;

1. Proprioception: It is a sense of the location of your body pats and the actions they do.
2. Equilibroception: This is a sense of balance that lets you know whether you are sitting, standing or lying down. It is found in the inner ear.
3. Nociception: It is a sense of pain.
4. Thermoreception: It is a sense of temperature.
5. Chronoception: It is a sense of the passage of time.
6. Interoception: It is a sense of internal needs like thirst, hunger etc.

MYTH 12: YOU'RE BORN WITH ALL THE BRAIN CELLS YOU'LL EVER HAVE, YOUR BRAIN IS HARDWIRED AND BRAIN DAMAGE IS ALWAYS PERMANENT

The heads of babies appear larger in relation to their body size than that of an adult and it is because of the imbalance between the brain and body growth during pregnancy. The brain of a newborn triples in size in the first year of their life and after that the rate of physical growth slows down. What continues to grow is the complexity of their neuronal networks as they go through pruning where unused synapses are cut to make room for more. This explains why the size of a person's head cannot be used to measure their intelligence. As the brain reaches half of its grown size by 9 months – almost 2 years old, a baby's head must be large and expand quickly to match the rest of the body's growth. The brain achieves its maximum size in females at 11½ years and in boys at 14½ years. At these ages it is not fully mature in terms of internal growth and executive functioning till 25 years.

As an adult, adding more information to your brain doesn't increase its size. What grows is the number of neurons and complexity of their network. While genes are likely to play a role in degeneration of synapses, some recent research focused on how a person's environment can have a significant impact on their pruning process. It is the nature versus nurture rule in action. Exercised synapses develop stronger while weaker synapses get weaker and are removed. We used to think that we were born with a specific amount of neurons for our entire lives and they cannot be replaced when destroyed; this is the same way many scientists thought the brain cannot be fixed after damage. The brain is plastic throughout life and it can reorganize itself in response to events. In the right circumstance, it can also produce new brain cells.

While neurogenesis has been demonstrated in other animals, it wasn't until the 1990s that scientists focused on demonstrating the creation of new brain cells in humans. In 1998, a Swedish neurologist, Peter Eriksson was the first person to publish a widely cited study demonstrating that in the hippocampus there is a reservoir of neural stem cells that is constantly refilled and can become brain neurons. In our lifetime, we all undergo development in specific portions of our brains. We can also rewire and physically reshape our brain. In reaction to events, learning or injury, the brain constantly reshapes itself. What you choose to focus your attention on structurally and functionally rewires your brain. The idea that humans may change our circuitry through neuroplasticity and that neurogenesis happens throughout our lives has sparked a revolution in neuroscience. If you are curious on how the brain generates new neurons, it is mostly thanks to a protein called Brain-Derived Neurotropic Factor (BDNF) which is encoded by a gene on chromosome 11. BDNF not only promotes neurogenesis but it also protects existing neurons and promotes the creation of synaptic connections between neurons.

It is important to remember that brain plasticity works both ways. It is as easy to make changes that hinder the memory, physically and mental capacities as it is to make changes that increase them. According to Dr. Michael Merzenich "Older people are pros at encouraging plastic brain change in the wrong way". By changing your actions and even your way of thinking, you may transform your brain for better or worse. Negative habits have neural maps that reinforce them. Negative thoughts and continual worrying might cause brain alterations that are linked to depression and anxiety. Repeated mental states develop into neural features. We choose and mold how our ever-changing thoughts will work moment by moment. We choose who we will be in the next moment and these decisions are imprinted in tangible form in our material selves.

SECRETS OF SUPERAGERS

Most people didn't win the genetic lottery to be a SuperAger which is someone who has an incredible ability to preserve a youthful brain into old age. They exhibit no age-related reduction in the size of brain networks linked to memory ability. Their outer cortexes are also very thick like adults in their forties. Scientists are trying to figure out how to make us all SuperAgers and they realize it is not all hereditary. Science is demonstrating that we can have a significant impact on the environment of our brain with our lifestyle choices. SuperAgers do not act like old people and they keep sharp with good habits.

HOW TO KEEP A SHARP MIND

These are the 5 pillars of brain health; Move, Discover, Relax, Nourish and Connect. AARP was the first to outline these pillars based on existing scientific evidences that they are critical to promoting excellent cognitive function across the lifespan. This is what they mean;

1. Move: Exercise is beneficial to both the body and the brain. Physical activity is the only thing that has been scientifically proven to promote brain health and performance. We may find a link between eating a nutritious food and having a healthier brain but the

link between physical and mental fitness is powerful. Movement boosts your brainpower by assisting in the growth, repair, maintenance of brain cells and making you productive and attentive throughout the day.

2. Discover: According to a 2014 study from the University of Texas, Dallas, adopting a new hobby can help improve the brain.

3. Relax: The brain just like your body also needs to relax. According to a group of MIT researchers, multitasking can inhibit your thinking. Stress is especially destabilizing. Relaxing entails doing stress-relieving activities and getting enough sleep on a regular basis.

4. Nourish: For a long time, the link between food and brain health has been unreliable but now there is proof that eating certain foods like whole grains, nuts etc. while avoiding others like sugar can help prevent memory and brain decline.

5. Connect: We already know crossword puzzles helps to build brain function but connecting with people does a better job. A study in 2015 shows that having various social networks can improve brain plasticity and preserve our cognitive abilities. Interacting with people helps reduce stress and boosts the immune system.

QUESTIONS / EXERCISE

How do you keep a sharp mind?

_____
_____
_____
_____
_____
_____

How often do you multitask and what benefits does it
have?

_____
_____
_____
_____
_____
_____

When was the last time you engaged in physical activity?

_____
_____
_____
_____
_____
_____
_____
_____
_____

What truths have you discovered about the brain?

_____
_____
_____
_____
_____
_____
_____

Personal Notes, Lessons and Action Plans

CHAPTER 4

THE MIRACLE OF MOVEMENT

This Chapter's Objectives

- Understanding the importance of regular movement.
- Making exercise a regular routine.
- Using movements to enhance your brain function.

CHAPTER SUMMARY

The most important thing you can do to enhance brain function is exercise. Despite the other risk you face, fitness could be the most crucial ingredient in surviving for as long as possible. Exercise is the only behavioral activity scientifically proven to induce biological responses that can improve the brain. Although we cannot say that exercise would correct cognitive deficiencies and dementia, evidence is increasing. Remember: A moving body tends to stay in motion. A lot of myths about the aging process are being debunked by research. Contrary to popular belief, we don't become significantly slower as we age until we reach the age of 70. We can gain a lot from low-intensity hobbies like walking.

THE PACE OF AGING

Exercise had a tremendous effect on brain function that in 2018, the American Academy of Neurology published new guidelines for doctors in choosing the best decisions for treating patients especially those with MCI which is a precursor to dementia. The subcommittee reviewed 8 medications that could help slow the progression of MCI to Alzheimer's and they concluded that no drug was effective. There are approved drugs for treating symptoms of Alzheimer's but none for MCI. The scientists however declared that exercise should be recommended. Lack of exercise has been noted to be the most important risk factor in cognitive decline and development of dementia. Exercise is an example of how the brain and body chooses to heal using movement.

Various imaging technologies help in measuring the changes in the brain under certain conditions and physical activity has the strongest evidence of favorable brain changes. Physical activity requires less than you think as just walking is enough. You must however exercise regularly for at least 150 minutes weekly and include interval and strength training. Interval training is alternating between increasing the levels of speed, intensity and effort. Strength training is the use of weights or your body weight for resistance and this helps the development of muscular growth, tone, balance and coordination. A lot of people tend to claim that there is no time for exercise but you need to make the time as this is about your health.

SMARTER AND BIGGER BRAINS IN MINUTES OF MOVEMENT

Exercise helps digestion, metabolism, muscle tone, strength and bone density. A lot of people see it a way to lose weight but it is more than that. It has the power to activate your smart genes, promote emotional stability and prevent depression and dementia. It also enhances your self-worth and confidence when you choose the right activity. How can you be smarter after effective movements on the brain using exercise? Exercise doesn't automatically infuse the brain with facts or advanced skills but it will enhance your brain in ways that makes you think more swiftly, clear and with better focus. This can be achieved using different direct and indirect consequences.

This has nothing to do with your physical habits. It has been proven that being inactive regardless of your body weight is twice as dangerous as obesity. When you are motionless, your circulation slows and your body consumes less sugar causing more sugar circulation in the body. Being stationary has negative impacts on blood fats, high-density lipoproteins, resting blood pressure and the satiety hormone leptin. Sitting causes muscles to go into a state of dormancy, with less electrical activity leading to atrophy and breakdown. The enzyme lipoprotein lipase which breaks down fat molecules in the blood is also slowed down resulting in more circulation of fat. As you metabolic rate reduces, you stop burning many calories. The good news is that if you're active, those few minutes of motion will reverse the consequences of sitting too much. While lack of exercise is linked to early sickness and death, basic movement has been found to protect against such an outcome.

MOVING THROUGH EVOLUTION

Humans have had to be physically active everyday to survive. Science proves that over the years our genome evolved in a state of constant movement and physical challenges as it took a lot of energy to find food and water. Basically, our genome expects and needs frequent movement as we are designed to be active down to our molecules. According to biologist and paleoanthropologist, Daniel E. Lieberman in a paper coauthored with Dennis M.

Bramble, we lived this long on earth due to our ability to move quickly. Our forefathers ensured our survival by tracking predators and hunting down prey for nourishment. They were able to acquire food and generate energy for mating allowing them to pass on their genes to the next generation of better humans. Dr. Liebermann made a compelling case in his 2013 book 'The Story of the Human Body' that our high levels of chronic diseases presently are the results of a change in our past and current lifestyle. In a follow up research in 2015, he lays out the contradiction saying "Humans developed to be adapted for regular, moderate quantities of physical endurance until their old age but humans were also selected to avoid excessive struggle". It is documented that a physician from Sushruta, an Indus Valley, was the first recorded doctor to recommend moderate daily exercises for his patients emphasizing that it should be done every day. It was more than 2.5 million years ago. He encouraged exercise because it made the body firm, light, supported muscle growth, enhance digestion and lowered decline.

BENEFITS OF EXERCISE

1. It helps to control blood sugar.
2. It helps lower the risk of inflammation which is important to prevent dementia.
3. Reduced stress
4. Increased levels of flexibility, strength and stamina.
5. Increased self-esteem
6. Reduced levels of blood sugar
7. Reduced risk for cardiovascular and high blood pressure.
8. It builds a stronger immune system.

SHAPE YOUR BRAIN BY GETTING INTO SHAPE

The biology of how exercise improves brain health goes beyond the idea that it improves oxygenated blood flow and delivers nutrients for neural cell maintenance and growth. There are two main ways in which exercise is beneficial to the brain. Exercise effectively utilizes blood sugar circulation and lowers inflammation while also increasing the production of growth factors which stimulate cell proliferation and function. These growth factors support the health of new neurons, blood vessel recruitment and survival of all neurons in the brain. Another way that exercise benefits the brain might be less objective but it is still significant. We know that regular movement reduces stress and anxiety while also enhancing sleep and mood which all have a good impact on the structure and function of the brain. These combined impacts contribute to long-term brain resilience while also allowing us to be more creative and perceptive in the short run.

Inner strength and mental fortitude are usually as a result of stress. When it comes to the positive effects of exercise on the brain, you've probably noticed that it reduces stress. When your body is stressed, the stress hormone cortisol is released, which is increasingly being blamed for long-term brain alterations. This is why young people who are exposed to chronic stress as children are more likely to develop mental health problems later in life.

According to studies, people with high blood sugar have a higher rate of cognitive deterioration than people with normal blood sugar. High blood sugar can lead to dementia for various reasons; it can weakened blood vessels in the brain increasing the risk of mini-strokes causing dementia and a large consumption of simple carbohydrates can make cells resistant to insulin especially those in the brain. As a result, brain cells are unable to absorb enough sugar to fuel their activity meaning that no matter how much food you consume, you brain could still be hungry. The same way blood sugar can be managed when you eat right and exercise, is the same way hypertension which is another risk factor for dementia can be managed. A study in 2014 on Americans by Rebecca Gottesman showed that having hypertension at midlife is a huge risk factor for cognitive decline. In 2017, she published a follow-up study which showed how certain risk factors increased your chances of eventually having dementia. Smoking and diabetes were the highest with diabetes at 77% and smoking at 41%. Hypertension followed with a 39% odd of dementia. Her work also showed how obesity doubled the risk of having elevates amyloid protein later on.

Another study done in 2018 used a more precise method to measure physical fitness when relating to brain health. During aerobic exercise, the researchers decided to assess the subjects' maximum oxygen intake. The test is called the VO2 max test. The subjects were made of healthy older people and people with minor cognitive impairment. The average age of the group was 65. All individuals were put through a battery of testing, including a treadmill VO2 max test, memory and reasoning assessment. The researchers also used advanced scanning technology to take an image of their brains to determine the integrity, and functionality of their white matter which carries information between the different parts of gray matter. White matter reflects how well the brain communicates and weak white matter means weaker connections throughout the brain which can happen with age. The findings of the study revealed a strong link between poor levels of aerobic fitness and weaker white matter in people with mild cognitive impairment. It was linked to reduced brain function explaining why these individuals performed poorly on memory and thinking exams. The researchers came to a conclusion that being physically fit is linked to having better white matter and better memory and thinking abilities is also linked to healthier white matter.

JUST AS YOU WOULD BRUSH YOUR TEETH

Exercise refers to a combination of aerobic cardio work, strength training, and flexibility and balance exercises. It includes being physically active at all times of the day. It is like brushing your teeth; it must be done every day. A lot of people overlook upper-body strength especially as they become older but it is beneficial to posture, bone density, metabolism and even the lungs to help fight pneumonia. All you need to do every day is regular exercise that makes your heart pump and muscles flex. Your heart rate should be up at least 50% above the resting baseline for at least 20 minutes of the 30 minutes done in 5 days. To get the most benefit, exercise for about 150 minutes a week.

QUESTIONS / EXERCISE

What are the benefits of exercise on the brain and body systems?

_____

_____

_____

_____
_____
_____
_____
_____
_____
_____
_____
_____
_____

What parts of your body do you focus on when exercising?

_____
_____
_____
_____
_____
_____

How often do you experience stress?

_____
_____
_____
_____
_____

Personal Notes, Lessons and Action Plans

CHAPTER 5

THE POWER OF PURPOSE, LEARNING AND DISCOVERY

This Chapter's Objectives

- Understanding the concept and importance of cognitive reserve.
- Maintaining your sense of purpose.
- Understanding the flow.

CHAPTER SUMMARY

People who retire early have an increased risk for dementia and other factors that increase dementia. A study showed that each year of work reduced dementia by 3.2% and this makes sense because staying engaged keeps people active physically, socially and mentally. This is to say that you should delay retirement as much as you can and when you retire, find stimulating activities to keep your brain busy. Continued learning, discovery and completion of complex activities help to sustain a sense of purpose in life and this makes you believe your life is important and has a direction.

KEEPING THE BRAIN PLASTIC

Active aging is more than just moving your body, you also need to move your brain and exercise it in ways that keeps it healthy. Recruiting your muscles through exercise increases overall health and exercising your brain improves your general brain health. However, there is correct and wrong way to do it. The right way helps you tap into the brain's ability to reinforce and remodel its networks. How does a person with a sick brain avoid cognitive decline? It is done through cognitive reserve or brain resiliency which involves staying engaged in life through stimulating activities.

THE BRAIN AND COGNITIVE RESERVE

The concept of cognitive reserve is controversial because it is hard to define. Cognitive reserve in practical terms is the brain's ability to improvise and navigate around obstructions that could prevent it from completing a task. Your brain can adapt how it works to find new paths, allowing you deal with obstacles that would have destroyed your health and function. Imagine your brain networks as a network of roads, see how the more roads you have, the more chances you have to change directions if a place is blocked and still get to your destination. The roads are cognitive reserve which develops over time due to learning and curiosity and the more you learn the more networks/roads you create.

The concept of cognitive reserve originated in the 1980s when some scientists in Department of Neurology at University of California discovered that some older people at a nursing home with no symptoms of dementia died and autopsy shows that they had advanced Alzheimer's. Their paper suggested that these people had enough brain supply to counterbalance the damage in their brain and continue to function normally. They also noted that these people had an increased brain weight and a higher number of neurons. According to researchers, a stronger cognitive reserve can help you function better and longer is you are subjected to unplanned events like stress, surgery etc. that can affect the brain. There are two types of cognitive reserve; neural reserve and neural compensation. In neural reserve, preexisting brain networks that have more capacity may be less susceptible to disturbance and in neural compensation, alternate networks may counterbalance any disturbance of existing networks. One of the most important goals is to create and maintain your cognitive reserve which can be accomplished by keeping your brain busy. Creating and maintaining cognitive reserve cannot be done in a day. Cognitive reserve is an indication of how much you have taxed your brain over the years through different activities. It explains why epidemiologic evidence suggests that people with a higher IQ have a lower risk of getting Alzheimer's disease as they force the brain to learn new information and apply it resulting in the formation of new neural networks and strengthening of old ones. Cognitive stimulation strengthens the brain's resistance to disease. Higher education may not have an impact on a person's cognitive reserve as anyone can improve their cognitive reserve at any age no matter their level of education just as new brain cells can develop at any time in the brain. While lifelong education appears to be protective against dementia, it is also a luxury available to people with better financial status, social interactions and employment prospects. It is difficult to figure out which protective variable has the most impact and they interact with one another. The best thing to do is to focus on lifelong learning as it is how you continue to build and maintain that resilience.

THE DEFINITION OF "COGNITIVELY STIMULATING" ACTIVITIES

So many people are wrong when defining cognitive stimulating activities. A lot of people especially older think challenging the brain with puzzles and games helps maintain and improve brain health but evidence doesn't support this line of thought. The working memory especially when distracted can be improved using brain-training movies and games. Although research has discovered that while they can help your brain develop better, their benefits do not extend to other brain processes like problem-solving which is also important for creating cognitive reserve. Research has always shown that new knowledge helps the brain especially if it is something you are interested in.

In 2016, a secondary review of a 10-year study funded by the National Institutes of Health found that speed training was more helpful than memory and reasoning activities in terms of reducing the risk of dementia. A total of 11-14 hours of speed training has been shown to reduce the risk of dementia by 29%. Researchers from the Institute on Aging and 6 research universities led a primary study calling it ACTIVE (Advanced Cognitive Training in Vital Elderly) and it was created to assess people's cognitive performance and their capacity to carry out important every day activities. 2802 adults were enrolled and assigned to one of the following control groups;

1. Group that received instructions on reasoning plans
2. Group that received instructions on memory plans
3. Group that was given speed training with the help of computer games.

A variety of cognitive and functional tests were used to assess functional loss in all groups at the start and during intervals of the study after the first year and third year, some persons received booster training sessions. Not only did the speed training group benefit the most but their benefits were dose-related meaning those who did more training sessions benefitted more. The researchers stated that the findings associated to lower dementia risk could be due to reverse causation meaning there may not be a direct cause and effect between speed training and lower dementia risk.

Researchers are realizing that video games if designed correctly have untapped promise for training the brain to be faster, stronger and better. Dr. Adam Gazzaley is a neuroscientist and inventor who support this theory. He is a pioneer in digital medicine and an unconventional person in brain optimization. He separates what actually works to increase brain performance from things that are just hype. He likes the power of programs that affect the mind, using the latest technologies to see the brain's functionality in real time, he is able to watch and take notes of changes in the brain as it undergoes stimulation by a video-based brain game which usually demands that a person avoids distraction and uses hand-eye coordination. He captures the areas of the brain that light up and are stimulated during this process and correlates them with what it means functionally for the brain. He believes that experience drives the brains plasticity and we can create experiences for this specific purpose to improve and protect brain function. His work got significant recognition and he also agrees that the power of video games should not be exaggerated.

A STRONG SENSE OF PURPOSE

Dozens of studies have found that elderly people who have a sense of purpose in life are less likely to suffer from dementia, Alzheimer's etc. They also have a bigger chance of living longer. Believing you have a purpose in life could lower your risk of dementia in future by 20%. With a sense of purpose, it is easier to be physically active and take care of yourself. It also aids stress management and reduces the risk of harmful inflammation. According to autopsies performed on adults in their eighties, people who thought their life had purpose significantly suffered less tiny infarcts which are little regions of dead tissue caused by restriction of blood flow. Having a sense of purpose can also help you keep your brain plastic and maintain your cognitive reserve. Purpose helps to combat depression which is a major risk for memory loss, stroke and dementia.

GETTING IN THE FLOW

There are many options for staying active and maintaining a sense of purpose. It is important that you choose activities that will allow you to "flow". We have all experience what it is like to be in the "flow", "zone" etc. The term "flow" is used to characterize these experiences. It shows that you are in a mental state where you are completely engrossed in an activity with no distractions. As you are absorbed in the action, you are deeply concentrated and experiencing a surge of energy. You are comfortable under pressure. The concept of the flow is recognized in many fields like arts, occupational therapy etc. you cannot be in the flow without a sense of purpose.

QUESTIONS / EXERCISE

How has being in the flow helped you in the past?

_____

_____

_____

_____

_____

_____

_____

_____

_____

How does a person with a sick brain avoid cognitive decline?

_____

_____

_____

_____

_____

_____

_____

What is the right way to keep your brain plastic?

_____

_____

_____

_____

_____

_____

_____

Personal Notes, Lessons and Action Plans

CHAPTER 6

THE NEED FOR SLEEP AND RELAXATION

This Chapter's Objectives

- Understanding the negative impact of lack of sleep.
- Unlocking strategies to good sleep and relaxation.
- Practicing mindfulness activities.

CHAPTER SUMMARY

Two-thirds of people in the modern world are sleep deprived. There has been a lot of false information produced on the issue of sleep. People who claim to be able to function on 4 hours of sleep have no idea what they are talking about and if they only sleep that much, there are at a higher risk of developing a variety of health problems. Dementia, depression, heart disease, memory problems etc. are all linked to insufficient sleep. It can also cause behavioral bias when making judgment. Sleep deprivation is not a badge of glory. Despite the trend among popular and important people, there is no evidence that successful people get less sleep. Your body clock is unchangeable and you should realize how important sleep is in your life and begin to prioritize it. Every night, we all need 7-8 hours of sleep.

Contrary to popular belief, sleep is not a state of brain idleness. It is an important time when the body replenishes itself in different ways that affect every system in the body. It is natural for sleep patterns to vary with age but poor quality of sleep is not normal with age. While sleep disorders like sleep apnea become more common with age, they can be addressed with lifestyle adjustments to promote sleep. Sleep apnea is caused by a fall of the airway when sleeping. The muscles in the back of the throat fail to keep the airway open causing pauses in breathing resulting in fragmented sleep. Sleep apnea is characterized by restless sleep and loud snoring. It can be treated using a continuous positive airway pressure (CPAP) device which is worn when sleeping. Because being overweight can aggravate sleep apnea, people who lose weight feel better and do not need the CPAP device.

SLEEP MEDICINE

Sleep medicine was unheard of a few generations ago but it is now a well-respected field of study that continues to educate us about the importance of sleep in maintaining optimal physical and mental health. Even the tiniest creatures require sleep and we mammals appear to be reliant on it. The amount and quality of sleep you obtain has a huge impact on your health. During sleep your body does not hit the pause button. Sleep is an important phase of regeneration and so it is more like a reset button. During sleep, billions of chemical operations take place at a cellular level to ensure that you see another day. A good night's sleep keeps you alert, creative, observant and capable of adequately processing information. Sleep patterns affect your metabolism, strength of your immune system, stress tolerance, learning ability etc. to combine the events in your brain and remember things. Sleeping for six hours or less a night reduces your daily alertness by a third and can damage your ability to drive or handle machinery.

Dr. William Dement at Stanford University Sleep Research Center is commonly known as the father of sleep science as he began to study sleep in the 1950s. In 1970, he opened the first sleep disorder clinic and sleep laboratory to study and treat Obstructive Sleep Apnea (OSA). OSA happens when the tissues at the back of the throat collapse and restrict the airway. It is caused by excess weight, big tonsils or even the shape of a person's throat. A person with sleep apnea pauses breathing for 10-60 seconds lowering blood oxygen levels and putting a strain on the heart. These micro-awakenings can occur hundreds of times a night, stopping a person from experiencing all sleep cycles including deep sleep. It is extremely widespread presently affecting over 20% of people in the U.S. OSA raises your chances of getting heart disease, diabetes, stroke and cancer. It also increases the risk of accidents and affects a person's quality of life. Dr. Dement's accomplishments in sleep science have made a way for modern sleep research.

The influence of sleep on our hormone cycles is undervalued and influential to our sense of well-being. Everyone has a circadian rhythm that encompasses our sleep-wake cycle, change in body temperature, rise and fall of hormones that are coordinated with the solar day. It happens every 24 hours but you do not feel okay if your rhythm isn't in sync with the solar day. Your sleep habits control your circadian rhythm. Normal hormone patterns are directed by a healthy circadian rhythm. Leptin and ghrelin are the main appetite hormones that control our eating behaviors. Ghrelin lets us know that we should eat while leptin tells us to stop. When you feel hungry right before going to sleep, it is probably a circadian rhythm that is out of sync. A study shows that people who slept for 4 hours a night for 2 days in a row experienced 24% increase in hunger and tend to want a lot of high calorie snacks and starchy food. This was probably because the body needed a quick energy boost in form of carbs and this will lead to weight gain increasing your risk of cognitive decline.

A WELL-RESTED BRAIN IS A HEALTHY BRAIN

Scientists have proposed several mechanisms for why sleep deprivation causes a brain fog making it difficult to concentrate or remember important information. One of the most current hypotheses regarding memory and sleep proposes that sleep aids in the triage of essential memories, ensuring that we remember the most important experiences. Sleep is necessary is for strengthening and recording our memories for following recollection. Sleep spindles have been shown to efficiently transport recent memories from the hippocampus's short term memory region to the neocortex hard drive. In other words, sleep cleans the hippocampus so that it can take in new information and comprehend it. This memory arrangement is impossible to achieve without sleep. Sleep deprivation affects more than just your memory; it also stops you from processing information in general. You're not just unable to remember things but you're also unable to analyze information. While we've long known that chronic poor sleep is linked to neurodegenerative disorders like dementia, new research suggests that this problem can develop years before a person is diagnosed. Basically, sleep issues could be a warning sign to a more serious ailment. Getting adequate sleep can help you avoid dementia in future.

There is still a lot to learn about the relationship between sleep and inflammation but there is sufficient evidence to show that lack of sleeps raises the risks and levels of inflammation. A single night of insufficient sleep can activate the inflammatory processes in the body especially for women. Continuous lack of sleep or insufficient sleep can be really harmful to the body. The myth that there is no problem with sleep aids is false. Although they help you fall asleep faster, they do not allow you experience the natural restful sleep needed by the body. Some sleep aids also increase the risk of dementia and brain decline.

THE RINSE CYCLE

Sleep has been found to have a washing effect on the brain. The lymphatic system removes waste and fluid from the body tissues. Lymph is a colorless fluid that transports hazardous waste and cellular debris through specialized capillaries and as they are removed through the lymph nodes, they are filtered with the lymphatic fluid returning to the bloodstream. For a long time, scientists believed that the brain lacked a lymphatic system and relied on waste slowly spreading from the brain tissue into the cerebrospinal fluid until a paper changed this notion in 2012. Subsequent papers also showed that a night of bad sleep can be linked with the accumulation of beta-amyloid in the brain.

A team in the University of Rochester showed that CSF flow through the brain increased in mice only when they are asleep. This fluid protects the central nervous system and removes waste. The team theorized that this flow could work the same way as the lymphatic system in the body. Sleep cleans the brain of metabolic waste in the same way it cleans the hippocampus. Sleep doubles as a declutterer and rubbish collector. After this study, other works have shown that the brain has a process to remove waste. A vicious cycle can develop as the brain's ability to cleanse itself and the body's ability to sleep deteriorates as it ages. In a 2014 study of the glymphatic system, researchers discovered that the drainage rate in older mice was 40% lower than in younger mice. While we cannot change some of the natural effects of aging, this information is important because sleep problems are common among the elderly and often ignored.

Dr. Kristine Yaffe a professor of psychiatry, neurology and epidemiology at University of California, San Francisco hears two common complains at her memory clinic. They either have difficulty falling asleep or staying asleep. People get tired during the day and are forced to take a nap.   Over a 5oyear period, she led series of studies on people who were over the age of 75. She found that people with interrupted sleep had more than double the risk of getting dementia later on. Majority of these people experience sleep apnea, sleep-disordered breathings etc. in their natural circadian cycle. Another problem is that Alzheimer's disturbs sleep. You can see how a harmful cycle can develop: Sleep deprivation prevents the brain from cleaning itself resulting in extra amyloid in the brain which can lead to Alzheimer's disease. The condition then pushes then pushes the brain down a path that leads to deterioration of sleep and this throws off the body's clock affecting a lot of systems negatively. The sleep disturbance is aggravated by a change in metabolism and important sleep-related hormones and the cycle continues. The damage gets worse until the cycle stops. Dementia doesn't just make it difficult to sleep; bad sleep may also contribute to the development of cognitive loss. Sleep is medicine; we need it to work during the day and recharge at night.

THE TOP TEN SECRETS TO SLUMBER

1. STICK TO A SCHEDULE AND AVOID LONG NAPS: Get up at the same time everyday even on weekends. Many people try to shift their sleep habits on weekends and make up for sleep deprivation during the week but this can disrupt a healthy circadian rhythm. You are likely to experience a social jetlag if you stay up on weekends to socialize and sleep the next morning. Irregular sleep habits are harmful to your health and research on if naps have an advantage on the brain of older people is still inconclusive. If you must nap, keep it to 30 minutes in the early afternoon as longer naps in the day can interfere with sleep at night. Although sleeping doesn't cause Alzheimer's, it may signal destruction of specific brain networks designed to keep you alert. The brain areas that promote alertness deteriorate when tau accumulates and this can happen very early. This could also explain why people with the disorder have a tendency to sleep excessively before experiencing other known symptoms.

2. DON'T BE A NIGHT OWL: The best time to sleep is just before midnight when you are really tired. in the early hours of the night, non-REM sleep mostly dominates the sleep cycle and as it gets late going closer to dawn, REM sleep takes hold. Non-REM sleep is deeper and more restorative than REM sleep despite the fact that both types of sleep are vital and have different advantages. It is important to keep in mind that as you get older, your ideal

bedtime may change. The older you get, the earlier your bedtime and the time you wake up naturally but ensure that the hours you spend sleeping remains the same.

3. WAKE UP TO EARLY MORNING LIGHT: To help set your body's clock, ensure you open your eyes to sunlight first thing in the morning. Mornings are important to our evolutionary biology and neuroscience; we are wired to wake up early and take in the rays of the sun.

4. GET MOVING: Regular exercise promotes good sleep. It can also help in achieving and maintaining healthy body size which allows you sleep better.

5. WATCH WHAT YOU EAT AND DRINK: avoid caffeine after lunch and don't eat or drink for 3 hours before bed to avoid waking up in between to go to the restroom. Heavy dinners can disturb when taken too close to bedtime and reduce your alcohol consumption.

6. MIND YOUR MEDICINES: Sleep-related chemicals can be found in drugs. Many regularly used drugs like antidepressants, steroids; beta-blockers etc. have side effects that might affect sleep. Be careful about the medications you take and if they are required, take them in the day if you can when they'll have lower effect on your sleep.

7. COOL, QUIET AND DARK: The best sleeping temperature is between 60-67 degrees Fahrenheit. Stay away from light sources like phones and sleep in the dark. If you cannot completely darken your environment, use a sleep mask and if you live in a noisy place use a sound machine or white noise generator to drown out the noise. Keep pets away from your bed.

8. ELIMINATE ELECTRONICS: The bedroom should be for sleeping and not looking at any form of screen especially your phone. Blue wavelengths are a good suppressor of melatonin, the hormone needed for sleep, they and stimulate the alert brain centers. Almost all lights artificial or natural contain blue wavelengths. The major issue is that LEDs which are present in TVs, phones and computers produce a lot of blue wavelengths. For optimal melatonin production, avoid blue light for a few hours before sleeping. Warm wavelengths of about 2700-3000K should be used in your house LED lighting. Instead of blue or green lights, make sure your clocks, nightlights and other electronic devices use red or warm glow lights. You can avoid blue lights on your device; you can get an app that alters the color temperature.

9. ESTABLISH BEDTIME ROUTINES: At least 30 minutes- 1 hour before you sleep, try to unwind and do things that lets your body know it is almost time to sleep. Stop stimulating tasks and indulge in relaxing activities like taking a warm bath, stretching etc. Keeping your feet warm by wearing socks also make it easier to fall asleep. Also avoid having tough conversations before bed.

10. KNOW THE WARNING SIGNS: If you have trouble falling asleep or staying asleep three times a week for at least 3 months, you may have a legitimate sleep disorder that needs treatment.

DON'T FORGET DAYTIME R&R

Sleep is a restorative activity that the body needs, but there is a difference between sleep and rest. To stay bright; we need sleep, rest and must incorporate different rest and relaxing activities to our routine. Our mental health can be affected by this and good mental health is linked to a lower risk of dementia. It is therefore important to tackle low mental health by reducing stress and increasing mental resilience. When we face a problem, we often let our emotions blur the practical solutions in front of us and this can be very frustrating. Through meditation, you can use logic and reason to clearly locate the issue and separate it from unrelated worries, allowing you to find a solution. It is a very simple process. Incorporating deduction and critical thinking in your life can change it for better. For the first 2 minutes create a thought bubble and let it float above you. This is usually the hardest part but it allows you to reach the flow state where 20-30 minutes can easily pass. This process allows you to view your issues logically and is an important way to get the rest you need daily which is different from sleep.

Mindfulness practices such as yoga and meditation are now used often even in the medical field. There is a common factor in these practices which is being present in the moment and monitoring the things going on in your life. It has been said a lot that mindfulness activities can help with managing stress but it is important to know that this theory has been researched adequately in the medical field. These habits are also used in military conflict zones. Mindfulness practices have been seen to reduce cortisol which is the stress hormone. Meditation has a long history but it was scientifically validated recently as researchers finally understand how it can influence the aging process. It started in 2005 when researchers at Harvard's Massachusetts General Hospital published an imaging study showing that people who meditated often possessed thicker cerebral cortex areas including the prefrontal area.

27 studies by the same group and others have confirmed that "thick-brained" people are smarter and have better memories. These areas are involved in attention, sensory processing and planning of complex cognitive tasks.

The relaxation response elicited by meditation can also be gotten through yoga, tai-chi, breathing exercises, progressive muscle relaxation etc. Deep breathing is useful because it produces a parasympathetic nerve response which is susceptible to stress and anxiety. When you are stressed, your sympathetic nervous system goes into overdrive causing cortisol and adrenaline level to skyrocket but the parasympathetic nervous system can initiate a relaxation response and deep breathing is one of the most effective ways to achieve this. Your heartbeat, breathing and blood pressure reduces when you are fully relaxed. Deep breathing is something that can be done at any place and time. If you have never meditated before, start with a deep breathing exercise twice a day to prepare you for more advanced techniques. All you have to do is relax your body by sitting comfortably on a chair or floor, closing your eyes and releasing all the tension in the different parts of your body. Inhale as deeply as you can through your nose, feeling your diaphragm and abdomen rise as your stomach expands. When you believe you have hit the top of your lungs, take a few more breaths. Exhale slowly to a count of 20, sucking every last breath out of your lungs and continue doing this at least 5 times.

Mindfulness can be achieved in different ways. It could be by using an app on your phone, going for a yoga class; Japanese forest bathing etc. Forest bathing recently became popular as way to reduce cortisol production and lower heart rate and blood pressure. When practicing this and taking in the air of the forest, you are also absorbing compounds called phytoncides which protects the trees from insects and other forms of stress. These phytoncides can also defend us by increasing our killer immune cells and reducing cortisol levels. While it has been recommended that people spend time in nature to boost their mental health, we now know what forest aroma does for the body and mind. You do not need to go to a forest to achieve this; you can dig the earth of your garden or go to a park. There is an old Indian concept of enjoying a joyful 100-year existence by spending the third stage of one's life in the forest as part of a peaceful lifestyle called Vanprastha (life as a forest-dweller). Walking in nature instead of cities has shown to help people manage stress, reduce over thinking and regulate their emotions.

These are some R&R ideas to consider for better mental health. These strategies help build a more productive brain.

1. Become a regular volunteer in your community: Think about helping and taking a leadership role in a group or organization you are part of as it has been shown that those who volunteer are likely to have less depression, anxiety and a sense of purpose.
2. Express gratitude: Think about the things you are grateful for at the beginning and end of your day. Keep a gratitude book. According to research, gratitude has been shown to reduce stress, anxiety and boost empathy and happiness. It is difficult to be angry or distressed when you are happy.
3. Practice the art of forgiveness: according to psychology research, this helps promote self-esteem and life satisfaction.
4. Look for things that make you laugh: Laughter causes the release of "feel good" hormones like endorphins,

dopamine and serotonin which can help reduce stress, anxiety and pain.

5. Take breaks from email and social media: Think about putting off your notifications. Put your phone on silent or another room to help you focus on a task. Set aside time to check social media and avoid using phones when eating and spending time with family. Mornings are the best time of the day; stay away from emails and use it to focus on your most creative work.

6. Find another hour in your day at least once a week: Be strict with the time spent on electronic devices. If you set aside a day to be without your devices, you'll have extra time to do other things you want.

7. Establish a system of rewards: The brain and body enjoy rewards and expecting one could cause a dopamine rush; this is why the Pomodoro technique is effective. It is a tried-and-true method for getting the most out of your time by rewarding yourself with tiny breaks at regular intervals. It is simple; choose a task and set your timer for 25 minutes. Concentrate on the task till the timer goes off and then take a 5-minute break before continuing.

8. Don't multitask- tackle your day like a surgeon: The brain does not like to manage numerous things at once despite our best efforts. Sure, you can walk and talk while eating your lunch but your brain cannot focus on two tasks that require thinking, comprehension and conscious effort at the same time. The brain handles tasks in a logical order but it may transfer attention between them so quickly that we have the impression that we can multitask. If you want to get more work done with less effort, build on your attention capacity by focusing and concentrating on one task at a time avoiding distractions. When you have worked for

awhile and you aren't getting anywhere, allow your mind to wander. You will not only accomplish more but you will experience a degree of joy that is hard to duplicate.

9. Identify your marbles and sand and plan accordingly: When filling a jar with marbles and sand, which should you put first? The marbles and then the sand can fill the gaps. This is a powerful metaphor for organizing your day and making the most of your time. See the marbles as the building blocks of your day (appointments, commitments, exercise, sleep) while the sand represents every other thing like checking your email, returning calls. Make sure not to get caught in the sand.

10. Declutter your life: Declutter closets, storage spaces etc. Donate any old clothes or books that you no longer use. Throw away unwanted letters, bills. Make it a habit to discard items that are not useful to you. Manage your surroundings as disorganization equals distraction and tension.

11. Set aside 15 minutes each day for yourself: Take advantage of this time to engage in stress-relieving activities. You could also spend this time to write in a journal and avoid distracting activities. The goal is to know yourself and a lot of people are not good at it.

12. Let yourself daydream: The mind cannot stay in one direction for an entire day. Instead of allowing your ideas to take control and run themselves, compel the brain to direct them as much as possible. Daydreaming can serve as a brain reset.

13. Do not be afraid to seek help from a health professional if you have concerns about your mental health: Mental health issues like anxiety and

depression are very common among people and can always be treated.

LIFE TRANSITIONS

It is crucial to recognize that we all go through different stages in life that present different problems. Transitions marked by events as the birth of a child, changes in finances, accidents etc. occur as people grow older. People who are able to adapt to changing life circumstances and experiences may be able to return to more normal feelings and mental states more quickly. Long-term melancholy is not a typical reaction to these things and it increases the risk of cognitive impairment. However, there is a silver lining to becoming older. Not everyone has to be unhappy as they grow older; most people report a higher level of mental health as they progress into their mid-fifties and later years. A U-shaped curve of happiness across the life span is generally defined as a tendency to report high levels of happiness and well-being around the age of 18-21, dropping during young adulthood and midlife, with considerable increases starting at age 50. People are happier when they are younger and older but their happiness declines as they get older.

It is critical that you do everything you can to monitor your mental health and get treatment when your stress levels are dangerously high. Despite the fact that experts do not believe that depression, especially in middle age, promotes dementia eventually, this subject is still researched. Depression is a risk factor for dementia but it is unclear is the link is casual or coincidental. People who get dementia who have a history of depression are more likely to develop new symptoms.

QUESTIONS / EXERCISE

What's your sleep routine?

_____

_____

_____

_____

_____

_____

How does your sleep pattern affect your daily life?

_____

_____

_____

_____

_____

_____

_____

_____

_____

_____

_____

_____

_____

_____

How often do express gratitude and how has it impacted you?

_____

_____

_____

_____

_____

_____

_____

_____

_____

_____

What mindfulness and relaxation activities you engage in?

_____

_____

_____

_____

_____

_____

_____

_____

_____

_____

Personal Notes, Lessons and Action Plans

CHAPTER 7

FOOD FOR THOUGHT

This Chapter's Objectives

- The importance of good diet on mental health.
- Learning the best diet for the brain.
- Understanding the relationship between the heart and the brain.

CHAPTER SUMMARY

There is a lot of debate on what foods are beneficial or harmful against certain diseases and most doctors never have the talk with their patients on what food they believe is scientifically okay for them. The problem is that there is a lot of information about this topic and experts cannot differentiate between facts and a person's opinion. However, there is evidence that how you fuel your body can help protect your brain but it is not about a particular diet; it is about the way you eat. The term "superfood" has no medical significance. It is a marketing word used by food businesses to sell, despite the fact that it indicates that a food has health advantages. Fresh blueberries and a handful of omega-3-rich nuts can be superfoods but be cautious of claims that they do something specific for the brain.

WHAT'S GOOD FOR THE HEART IS GOOD FOR THE BRAIN

The quote "What is good for the heart is good for the brain" is not entirely true but some common conditions like high blood pressure, diabetes etc. harm both the heart and brain. Recent studies have linked decrease in dementia to an improvement in cardiovascular health. The heart-brain link extends beyond the fact that the brain receives blood from the heart. It is important to remember that the brain works in its own way mostly independent of the rest of the body. The blood-brain barrier serves as a gated door allowing only certain molecules important to neuronal function to enter the brain from the blood. This is what allows the brain to function independently to some extent.

Dr. Richard Isaacson, the director of Alzheimer's Prevention Clinic at Weil Cornell was taught to be crazy by the dean of the medical school when he tried to establish a prevention clinic for Alzheimer's. However, times have changed and presently there are various clinical trials done to achieve the same goal. The FINGER study led by Dr. Mila Kivipelto was completed in 2014 and showed that a 2-year combination therapy which targeted things like a good diet and exercise can help preserve cognition. Dr. Isaacson however is creating his mark in this unexplored field. His credentials impressed the Cornell dean who was ready to let him do the screening as he was so young and now he is in charge of people who build applications to help his work and develop new methods of cognitive testing. In 2011, his work demonstrated that basic lifestyle modifications can delay progression of cognitive impairment due to aging process by an average of 2-3 years. Alzheimer's starts in the brain years before the first symptoms of memory loss occurs, giving people at risk time to prevent it by making healthy brain choices. His research revealed that patients can be proactive and engage with their doctors to improve their cognitive performance while also lowering the risk of

Alzheimer's and heart issues. He prescribes certain foods to his patients as he understands the importance of nutrition and he notices a difference in their outcomes due to this. His approach is similar to treating other chronic diseases and he takes a fresh approach to the standard ways of controlling the disease. Every patient needs an individual plan to prevent and treat their dementia as people are different. He prefers focusing on prevention because he knows the disease starts before the signs begin to show.

The idea of preventing and reducing symptoms of Alzheimer's started in the 21st century. What you eat could be one of the most important factors affecting your brain's health presently and in the future. You eat everyday and the way your body reacts to what you eat has an impact on your entire body physiology. While no single item will guarantee optimal brain health, a variety of healthful foods can help protect the brain from harm, and it's never too early to start. The food to eat as a child can begin to lay the groundwork for protecting your brain later in life. It should come as no surprise that the normal Western diet is not a brain-friendly, being heavy in salt, sugar, extra calories and saturated fats. According to the findings, eating a plant-based diet rich in a range of fresh fruits and vegetables, is linked to improved brain function. Increasing fruit consumption by a serving per day can reduce your chance of dying from a cardiovascular event by 8%. Eating healthy entails consuming real food rather than taking pills and supplements. While we all like the concept of a pill that contains all of the micronutrients in one convenient packaging, this method is neither effective nor feasible. Evidence demonstrates that when micronutrients like vitamins and minerals are ingested as part of a balanced diet, they provide the greatest benefit because all of the other nutrients in healthy food help the micronutrients to be better absorbed and do their work. While there are certain star players, they aren't as effective without the support of the other elements.

You should strive to create a style of eating you can easily maintain. It requires learning new methods of shopping and finding new foods. Stop outside attack on your brain by reducing sugar intake, highly salty foods, processed meat, fast food intake etc.

MY GUIDE TO GOOD EATING

No particular food functions as a savior for promoting or maintaining brain health; health advantages are determined by a combination of foods and nutrients in our food.

S: Slash the sugar and stick to your ABCs

We all need to reduce our sugar intake. It is the easiest way to start eating healthy. Sugar intake relates to the brain in so many ways. In part 1, Alzheimer's was introduced as type 3 diabetes and we noted how control over blood sugar makes your brain better. High blood sugar can be sneaky in people with normal weight but it is a must for obese people. Excess fat makes people insulin resistant and the fat releases hormones and proteins that cause a rise in inflammation in the brain which equals cognitive deterioration. When you follow your ABCS, you reduce your sugar consumption reducing the risk of dementia and blood sugar imbalance. Sugar from processed food is not the same as sugar from natural foods. Artificial sugar is not a good replacement as the body cannot digest them properly. A paper in 2014 showed that artificial sweeteners affect the bacteria in the gut causing metabolic dysfunction like diabetes. Avoid sugar substitutes and reduced the intake of refined sugars. This means removing cookies, pastries, baked desserts etc. from your regular diet. Be wary of products labeled "diet" or "lite" because itt means they contain artificial sweeteners. The best foods are wholefoods. The ABCs allow us discern quality foods (A-listers), food we should include (B-listers) and food we should reduce (C-listers)

A-LIST FOODS TO CONSUME REGULARLY: Fresh vegetable, whole berries (not juice), fish and seafood, healthy fats like avocado, nuts and seeds.

B-LIST FOODS TO INCLUDE: Beans and other legumes, whole fruits, low sugar, poultry and whole grains.

C-LIST FOOD TO LIMIT: Fried food, sugary foods and pastries, processed foods, red meat and red meat products, whole fat dairy high in saturated fat and salt.

H: Hydrate Smartly

When we get older, our ability to perceive thirst reduces which is why older people are usually dehydrated. A good rule to know is when you feel thirsty; you have stayed too long without water. We frequently confuse hunger with thirst. Even mild dehydration can deplete your energy and disrupt your mental rhythm. We need to eat when food is available as the brain cannot differentiate hunger and thirst which is why we are constantly overstuffed and dehydrated. Researchers have discovered that even mild dehydration is linked to confusion, disorientation and cognitive impairment. The severity of dehydration affects thinking skills. The best thing to do is to drink lots of water. You can also take coffee or tea in the morning. Caffeine is where most people get their antioxidant fix. Several studies have established a link between coffee and tea consumption and a lower risk of cognitive decline and dementia. The reason is not evident but it is known that short-term effects of caffeine include increase in alertness and cognitive performance while the long-term effects are still hard to understand. Several studies have found that those who consume coffee have greater cognitive performance over time than people who don't. However, it is possible that the caffeine or compounds in tea and coffee aren't the cause of this improvement but it is as a result of better education or health. Consuming coffee or tea won't hurt your brain unless you are drinking huge amounts of caffeinated energy drinks with your coffee.

Although alcohol is not a source of hydration, it can be included in a balanced diet. While there is strong evidence that moderate use of alcohol can have heart-health and brain-health benefits, several researches suggest that alcohol consumption might also have negative effects on the brain. Moderate amounts of alcohol have been related to detrimental brain health effects in some people. There will always be a debate on the risk-benefit analysis on alcohol but if you do not take it don't start in order to protect your brain and if you do, don't take in excessive quantities.

A: Add more Omega-3 Fatty Acids from Dietary Sources

Omega-3 fatty acids are abundant in fatty fish like sardines and wild meat like cattle, deer etc. Plant-derived oils and seed are also good sources of omega-3 fatty acid. They are best obtained through food instead of supplements. Some research show that omega-3 supplements had no likelihood of reducing heart attacks in older people and other studies have shown that taking too much fish oil have negative effects like increased blood sugar levels and risk of bleeding. DHA (docosa-hexaenoic acid) is the most common omega-3 fatty acid in the brain and it has been shown to have a critical role in the maintenance of neuronal membranes. We should all try to eat more fish but be careful about where they came from as fish from polluted waters could have high mercury content which is harmful to the brain.

R: Reduce portions

Portion control is very vital as it is a strong preventive strategy. The easiest way to do this is to make your meals yourself and ensure you do not go back for seconds. Research also agrees that taking a lot of home-made meals leads to a better diet. We also need to consider the impact of the method of cooking on our health. Slow, low temperature cooking is better compared to fast, high temperature cooking like frying. Frying can produce harmful chemical compounds that could promote inflammation harming the brain. Avoid mystery oils and sauces when cooking.

Intermittent fasting has gained popularity recently as a way to reduce calorie consumption. There are 2 common approaches when it comes to fasting; eat few calories on specific days, then eat normally on other days and eating at certain times and not eating at other times. While long-term research on the advantages of fasting cannot be found, animal models show it can reduce the course of certain age-related disorders and improve cognition and mood. It has also been demonstrated to increase insulin sensitivity, which is beneficial to metabolism and brain health.

P: Plan Ahead

Don't let yourself get hungry and turn to junk food. When you get hungry and you are unprepared, your animal impulses lead you down the wrong path making quick and pleasant foods appealing. Try to plan your main meals in advance and ensure you shop ahead. Your shopping should include fruits and vegetables, beans and legumes, whole grains and seeds. Fiber is important to brain health as it changes the chemistry of a meal. When you don't eat enough fiber, your carbohydrates are absorbed more quickly, elevating your glucose and insulin levels possibly causing inflammation. Fiber consumption has been long linked to a reduced risk of depression, hypertension and dementia. It has also been linked to general healthy aging. There are two types of dietary fiber; soluble and insoluble. Soluble fiber is found in oats, peas, beans and citrus fruits. Soluble fiber dissolves in water to form a gel that decreases glucose and cholesterol levels. Insoluble fiber doesn't dissolve; roughage is what keeps the other digestive juices moving through your intestines. Insoluble fibers include nuts, whole grains, vegetables like green beans etc. It is stays intact as it moves through the digestive system. The best way to more fiber into your food is to plan ahead.

ADDITIONAL TIPS

ORGANIC? GRASSFED?

There is no proof that eating organic food gives more nutrition that normally grown food. A lot of people are

95

concerned about how pesticides, hormones and antibiotics can have adverse effects on the health. Some conventionally grown foods tend to have higher traces of pesticide so ensure to wash them properly and remove the back if possible. For beef, grass-fed cattle tend to have less fat which is better for the brain.

SPICE IT UP

Turmeric is a common spice especially in the Indian heritage. The main active ingredient in turmeric is curcumin. Curcumin is also used in Indian and Chinese medicine. Laboratory studies how curcumin has anti-inflammatory, anti-oxidant, anti-fungal and anti-bacterial activities and the prevalence of dementia is lower in communities where it is used frequently to cook.

THE GLUTEN DEBATE

Gluten is the main protein component of wheat, rye and barley. It can also be found in other foods like bread, pasta etc. A gluten-free diet is the only known treatment for celiac disease and when consumed by such patients it can lead to abdominal pain, diarrhea and other uncommon symptoms like headaches, fatigue etc. When constantly exposed to gluten these patients can be exposed to cognitive problems like memory difficulties and word finding. This is referred to as Brain Fog. Other people without celiac disease experience this brain fog and they are said to have non-celiac gluten sensitivity. Despite the widespread belief that gluten causes cognitive issues, there is no evidence that it affects mental performance in those who do not have celiac disease or gluten sensitivity. Gluten-rich diets have not been connected to an increased risk of heart attack.

QUESTIONS / EXERCISE

What have you considered as superfood in the past?

_____

_____

_____

_____

How often do you consume sugar and sugary products?

_____

_____

_____

_____

What are the A-listers, B-listers and C-listers in your current diet?

_____

_____

_____

_____

_____

_____

How often do you hydrate?

_____

_____

_____

Personal Notes, Lessons and Action Plans

CHAPTER 8

CONNECTION FOR PROTECTION

This Chapter's Objectives

- Understanding the positive effects of relationships on the brain.
- Maintain good relationships.
- The positive and negative effects of social media.

CHAPTER SUMMARY

The health of a spouse is critical to the health of the other. The impact of personal relationships on a person's health has been studied from a physical and psychological view. People who lose their spouse have a 41% greater risk of death in the first 6 months. Relationships have been discovered to be associated with a range of physiological functions relating to the cardiovascular, endocrine and immune system. There is also a lot of data to back up the fact that we need a social connection to thrive especially when it comes to the brain health. According to research, having close relationships and engaging in meaningful social relationships can help keep your mind bright and memories strong. It isn't about how many connections you have; your brain processes can be influenced by the type, quality and purpose of your relationships. They have an impact on your risk.

Staying sociable and engaging in meaningful interactions with people can help protect the brain from the negative consequences of stress. In our society, social isolation and feelings of loneliness are on the rise. We are superconnected through social media but are growing apart as a result of a lack of true connection and medicine is realizing that this lack of connection has serious emotional, physical and mental effects particularly among the elderly. A survey revealed that 20% of people over the age of 40 are socially isolated. This is significant because adults who were satisfied with their friends and social activity were more likely to report an improvement in their memory and thinking skills over the past 5 years while those who were unhappy with their social lives reported the opposite. The damaging effects of social isolation tend to start early.

THE SECRET SAUCE TO A LONG, SHARP LIFE

Being wealthy or famous is not what makes a person happy and healthy; healthy relationship does. A good relationship kills loneliness making people happier and healthier. Socially isolated people often have health declines in their midlife causing a decline in their mental health. A committed relationship is not about the number of friends you have but about the quality of the relationship. Being a committed relationship in your eighties tends to protect the brain according to a Harvard study. A good relationship isn't always good at all times but as long as the people in it feel secure, the brain is not at risk of a decline. Although social media can be lonely, it gives people the opportunity to engage socially especially for people living in remote areas. Social media allows people to communicate freely and increase their confidence which can be beneficial to mental health.

TIPS TO STAYING SOCIALLY ENGAGED

1. Focus on relationships you enjoy.
2. Try to connect with people regularly. It could be digitally or physically.
3. Keep relationships with people of all ages.
4. Have at least a trusted friend to communicate with frequently.
5. Think about adopting a pet and reach out to professionals in time of need.

QUESTIONS / EXERCISE

How do you build meaningful relationships?

_____
_____
_____
_____
_____
_____
_____
_____
_____

When was the last time you experienced a good relationship?

_____
_____
_____

_____

_____

_____

_____

_____

How has social isolation affected you personally?

_____

_____

_____

_____

_____

_____

How has the loss of a loved one affected your mental
health?

_____

_____

_____

_____

_____

_____

_____

_____

Personal Notes, Lessons and Action Plans

CHAPTER 9

PUTTING IT ALL TOGETHER

This Chapter's Objectives

- Changing your habits.
- Using previous lessons to achieve a better lifestyle.
- Evaluating your progress.

CHAPTER SUMMARY

Changing certain habits can be a challenge especially if it is something that you do often. It is hard at first but eventually you have no problem doing it. The program below will be done for 12 weeks and it will help you address the important areas needed to improve your brain health while simultaneously establishing a new habit a week.

WEEK 1 AND 2: DIVE INTO THE FIVE

The following areas can be addressed in the next 2 weeks;

MOVE MORE

If you exercise regularly, continue while also trying to add new moves to reach new muscles. You can also try new forms of exercise. Try to increase workouts to 30 minutes a day, 5 days a week. Engage in strength training for 2-3 days and avoid doing it back-to-back giving your muscles time to recover. On days you feel lazy, go for walks or take restorative yoga classes. If you do not exercise regularly, start with 5-10 minutes of burst exercise and work for 20 minutes at least 3 times a week. This can be achieved in different ways. If there is no time for exercise, find ways to get in extra minutes of physical activity. Limit the time spent sitting. Move around more for the benefit of your body and brain.

LOVE TO LEARN

Read books, join writing classes, and learn new skills and topics. These are ways to keep your brain active.

SLEEP HYGIENE

For someone who gets less than 6 hours of sleep every night, increase it to at least 7 hours. This is the bare minimum to have a functioning brain and body. If you don't know how to cultivate good sleeping habits, start with timing your meal well and following a routine for your bedtime.

Also pick a relaxation activity for at least 15 minutes to reduce stress.

EAT SANJAY STYLE

When you eat is also as important as what you eat. Try to eat only when the sun is out. Eat more in the morning and less at night. If possible, reduce snacking. Follow the SHARP program to help improve your diet.

S: Slash the sugar.

H: Hydrate smartly.
A: Add more omega-3 from natural sources
R: Reduce your portions
P: Plan meals ahead

BUILDING A BETTER BREAKFST

Instead of cereals, pastries etc. eat better foods. Skip juices, smoothies etc. and replace them with tea or coffee. Drink to hydrate.

SMARTER LUNCHING

Avoid fast foods and highly processed lunch. Take water instead or unsweetened tea instead of soda and sugary drinks. These same rules also apply to dinner and try to avoid having dessert.

CONECT WITH PEOPLE

If you are socially active, keep it up. For socially isolated people, ensure you call a person often to either hang out or just talk.

WEEK 3 AND 4

Make your routine better by choosing at least 2 options;

1. Going for a 20-minute power walk after lunch most days.
2. Invite a neighbor for dinner
3. Have 2 of your food feature cold-water fish.
4. Get a meditation app if you do not have.
5. Eliminate soft drinks if you still take them

WEEK 5 AND 6

Choose 3 options to add to your routine;

1. Keep a gratitude journal if you do not have one. Spend 5 minutes a day writing at least 5 people or situation you are grateful for. It is okay to repeat things on the list.

2. Add an extra 15 minutes to tour exercise routine.
3. Try yoga or pilates class or go on a hike with someone.
4. Avoid processed foods.
5. Add a relaxation activity to your bedtime routine.

WEEK 7 AND 8

Add more to your routine by doing the following;

1. Try volunteering in the community.
2. Buy fresh foods.
3. Schedule a checkup with your doctor if you haven't had one in at least a year.
4. Write a letter to younger person in your family explaining an important lesson you've learnt in life.
5. Read books on topics that interests you but you've never read before.

WEEK 9 AND 10

Ask yourself these questions to rate your progress over the past weeks and if you cannot answer them positively, reread the chapter that covers the issues you have. If you are not getting the desired results, seek professional help.

WEEK 11

Think about how you want people close to you to deal with a diagnosis of dementia. It is important to have these conversations to be prepared. Talk to your loved ones, write how you would want it to be handled.

WEEK 12

Make a list of the things you did differently and evaluate what worked and what didn't and areas that need improvement. Use this week to plan ahead and have a deep talk with a friend while on a walk. Create activities that are non-negotiable and follow them strictly. Be flexible but consistent as the brain is not a machine and when you default in your program, cut yourself some slack and try to get back to the routine. Write down your motivating goals.

QUESTIONS / EXERCISE

How hard is it for you to follow a routine?

_____

_____

_____

_____

_____

How do you react to falling out of a routine?

_____

_____

_____

_____

_____

_____

_____

How often do you go for medical checkups?

_____

_____

_____

_____

_____

Personal Notes, Lessons and Action Plans

CHAPTER 10

DIAGNOSING AND TREATING AN AILING BRAIN

This Chapter's Objectives

- Knowing the various symptoms of cognitive dysfunction.
- Understanding the importance and effects of early detection.
- Finding help.

CHAPTER SUMMARY

Dementia tends to feel like war as there are numerous casualties including the patient, their caregivers and their families. It costs a lot to manage and can also be emotionally and physically draining. The approach for the treatment of dementia has changed over time; it no longer focuses on desperation but improvement in the care process, early diagnosis and enabling the patients live well.

BRINGING HOPE

A lot of people tend to ignore the early signs and warning of dementia until it is advanced and too late. No symptom is too small to neglect or ignore. Being diagnosed with dementia can be really hurtful and painful but it doesn't have to be a shameful thing. It helps to engage with other people, trying to remain as active and social as possible till the very end. Try to find ways to manage your symptoms as they progress; it could be listening to recordings or writing to help you remember things easily. Knowing that they are people with this disease living their lives as best as they can is a beacon of hope for others.

A POUND OF PREVENTION

The best way to treat dementia is to prevent and as discussed previously there are ways to reduce the risk of getting the disease which also help improve quality of life when diagnosed with the disease. Alzheimer's starts 20-30 years before symptoms start to show and this gives people an opportunity to work on preventing the disease. The space between brain changes and presence of symptoms is called the preclinical time. Researchers work with the mindset that if you cannot entirely prevent the illness, you can try to delay it for as long as possible and this is also a mindset we should have. Recommendations such as eating certain ways, engaging in physical activities and other changes in lifestyle are natural ways of preventing and beating the disease for people who have it.

Dr. Isaacson has an approach called the ABCs of Alzheimer's prevention. A is for anthropometrics, B is for blood biometrics and C is for cognitive performance. This allows him to design treatment strategies as he assesses the patients regularly. People who address their fundamental biology are more likely to respond to traditional treatments and this can be done by any doctor. Techniques like the Keep Sharp strategy can be used to prevent end ensure a better life for people with Alzheimer's disease.

THE THREE STAGES OF ALZHEIMER'S DISEASE

Alzheimer's disease involves 3 stages; the mild/early stage, the middle/moderate stage and the late/severe stage. The stages can also be broken down into 7 phases from 1 which signifies no impairment to 7 which signifies a very severe decline. On an average, an Alzheimer's patient lives for 4-8 years after diagnosis but it can be more as people vary. These are the stages of Alzheimer's diseases as defined by the Alzheimer's Association;

EARLY STAGE: MILD ALZHEIMER'S DISEASE

In this stage, the person can still function on their own. They can perform regular tasks like driving, working etc. The person begins to notice memory lapses and with time other people start to notice it too. This stage is also called Mild Cognitive Impairment especially when the cause of dementia is not known. Doctors can detect the memory problems by asking specific questions. Common difficulties are losing valuable objects, difficulties in finding the right word, problems with remembering names etc.

MIDDLE STAGE: MODERATE ALZHEIMER'S DISEASE

This is usually the longest stage and symptoms become more significant and patients require more care. Patients have difficulties in performing certain tasks even if they can still remember things about themselves. Damage to the nerve cells in the brain makes it hard to communicate and perform tasks. Symptoms in this stage include;

1. Trouble controlling the bladder.
2. Changes in sleep patterns.
3. Wandering
4. Personality and behavioral changes

5. Forgetting etc.

LATE STAGE: SEVERE ALZHEIMER'S DISEASE

Symptoms in this stage become severe. Patients lose control of their movements and awareness. Communication becomes difficult and there are noticeable personality changes. Other symptoms include vulnerability to infections, forgetting people and things etc.

There is no test to determine the presence of Alzheimer's disease and even if a brain scan is done there are no parameters for normal and abnormal buildup of amyloid in the brain. Healthcare professionals find it hard to diagnose Alzheimer's until it is in the advanced stage with very visible symptoms. Most doctors hesitate to diagnose Alzheimer's as they believe nothing can be done to prevent the disease. Diagnosis is established with the help of neurologist, psychologists or geriatric psychiatrists. A standard medical workup for this disease consists of an MRI or a CT scan. A PET scan can also be used to show patterns of brain activity.

DEMENTIA MIMICS

NORMAL PRESSURE HYDROCEPHALUS (NPH)

Symptoms include a gradual buildup of CSF, walking and balance problems, memory difficulties and urinary incontinence which is why it can be mistaken for dementia. It is treated by draining the excess amounts of CSF to mitigate the symptoms. However, this treatment doesn't work for everyone.

MEDICATIONS

People tend to take drugs for different reasons and do not consider the side effects of taking such medications. Some side effects tend to mimic Alzheimer's and can trigger cognitive decline. As we get older, the body finds it hard to efficiently metabolize these drugs allowing them to build up and possible affect cognitive function. Examples of such drugs are narcotic painkillers, muscle, relaxants, steroids etc. This is exactly why your doctor should know about every drug you take including supplements.

Anticholinergics side effects tend to mimic dementia so closely. They are substances that block the neurotransmitter acetylcholine in the central and peripheral nervous system. This neurotransmitter is needed for the transfer of signals between specific cells that affect specific body functions. In the brain, it helps learning and memory and in order places it aids muscle contractions. Effects of anticholinergics can make a person treat conditions like depression, epilepsy, Parkinson's etc. if you use anticholinergics, let your doctor know in order to weigh your options and find possible alternatives as the long-term effects are still unknown.

DEPRESSION

Severe depression tends to cause symptoms of dementia called psuedodementia. Cognitive impairment becomes better when the depression is treated but the peron still has a high risk of dementia when they get older. People with dementia also have a high risk for depression especially due to damage of the emotional circuitry in the brain. This is why it is important for people suffering from dementia to check for depression.

URINARY TRACT INFECTION (UTI)

They are caused by buildup of bacteria in the urinary system leading to infections. They present differently in older people mimicking symptoms of dementia like agitation, confusion, hallucinations etc. UTI-induced confusion also occurs in dementia patients. Appropriate treatment can help ease the symptoms

VASCULAR DEMENTIA

It is caused by carious cardiovascular issues such as a stroke. Mini-strokes are called subcortical vascular dementia and can make a person show signs of cognitive decline without showing signs of stroke. Treatment plan for this illness is improving diet, regular exercise, controlling blood pressure and participating in cognitive rehabilitation. Vascular dementia is also caused by damaged blood vessels in the brain due to diabetes, high blood pressure etc.

BRAIN TUMOR

Tumors can press on certain parts of the brain causing cognitive dysfunction. However, some of them can be removed allowing for better cognitive function. It is important that these tumors are identified and diagnosed early so increase the chances of the cognitive dysfunction being reversed. The longer they stay, the harder it is to remove.

SUBDURAL HEMATOMA

This happens when abnormal bleeding in the head causes blood to collect between the dura matter and the brain. Pressure from this buildup can cause symptoms of dementia. The hematoma can be drained surgically and small ones tend to go away on their own over time. The blood collections tend to accumulate as a result of frequent minor head injuries.

ALCOHOL MISUSE

Alcohol-related dementia is caused by long-term and excessive intake of alcohol. This can destroy the brain cells in areas critical for cognitive function. Excess drinking can also lead to other injuries that could cause cognitive dysfunction. It can also occur by combinig specific medications with alcohol.

THE MEDICAL WORKUP

It should contain a review of;

1. A person's medical history and complete physical with lab work
2. History of cognitive and behavioral changes
3. Current and past illnesses
4. Medications, diet and supplements
5. Lifestyle habits

Tests used to identify potential problems of Alzheimer's include;

1. Alzheimer's Disease Assessment Scale – Cognitive Subscale: it is a widely used test. It is used in cognitive research and drug trials. It measures memory, language and orientation. It consists of 11 sections and takes 30-35 minutes to complete. The scores for each section is added and the greater the score, the higher the dysfunction.
2. The Mini-Mental State Exam: it is also called Folstein Test and is a questionnaire that takes about 10

minutes to finish. It checks attention, language, recall, ability to obey simple commands and orientation. The lower the score, the higher the stage of dementia.

3. The Mini-Cog Test: takes 3 minutes to complete and have 2 components; a 3-iyem recall test for memory and a clock-drawing test.
4. Self-Administered Gerocognitive Examination: it asks important questions to evaluate how well the brain works. It takes 15 minutes.

NATIONWIDE PROGRAMS: WHERE TO FIND HELP

Alzheimer's Association is the leading voluntary health organization for Alzheimer's care and support. It helps with education, support and services for patients and their families. It collaborates with other research centers such as;

1. AARP which keeps a comprehensive library of resources for patients and caregivers. By answering 3 questions, caregivers can get information and resources for their concerns.
2. The Cleaveland Clinic's Lou Ruvo Center for Brain Health: it provides diagnosis and treatment options for patients and their families.
3. Dementia Action Alliance: it helps to take the stigma and misconceptions out of dementia.

THE FUTURE

A lot can be done to prevent cognitive impairment and this is why early detection is important. It allows families and patients to plan ahead for the best course of action financially and so on. Early detection should enable a patient and not disable them. It allows the patients live a good life as they still have a lot to offer and are not restricted by their illness. Patients can do a lot to improve their lives and allowing them engage in planning their care helps caregivers know the best options to enable health improvements and management. Delaying the occurrence of dementia by 5 years can drastically reduce its incidence rate and over the next few years these rates should be better as there would be significant improvements and finding through research and early detection techniques.

TREATMENTS: DRUG-BASED AND PEOPLE-BASED

Dementia is a complicated disease which makes it hard to treat. Two drugs have been approved to combat the disease and lessen symptoms; however, they do not completely cure the diseases. These drugs include;

1. The first class of drugs consist of cholinesterase inhibitors which breakdown acetylcholine and keep it at healthy levels. In clinical trials, they have shown some effects against functional and cognitive decline of people with Alzheimer's. drugs like this include Aricept, Exelon etc.
2. An NMDA receptor antagonist: this works by keeping communication channels of the brain cells open. It regulates the activity of glutamate in the brain. Glutamate is important because when brain cells get damaged by the disease, they pump out the excess which damages more brain cells.

These 2 drugs are usually prescribed together at the later stages of Alzheimer's. Other drugs can be prescribed to help with individual symptoms. Treatment for this disease doesn't always come in form of drugs; it can be in form of care and lifestyle changes.

QUESTIONS / EXERCISE

How do you differentiate the various stages of Alzheimer's?

_____

_____

_____

_____

_____

_____

_____

_____

_____

How open are you with your doctors about your lifestyle habits?

_____

_____

_____

_____

_____

_____

_____

What is the best mode of treatment for cognitive decline?

_____

_____

_____

_____

_____

_____

_____

_____

_____

_____

_____

Outline some factors that influence cognitive decline

_____

_____

_____

_____

_____

_____

_____

_____

_____

_____

_____

_____

_____

_____

Personal Notes, Lessons and Action Plans

CHAPTER 11

NAVIGATING THE PATH FORWARD FINANCIALLY AND EMOTIONALLY, WITH SPECIAL NOTE TO CAREGIVERS

This Chapter's Objectives

- Dealing with Alzheimer's.
- Taking care of yourself as a caregiver.
- Overcoming negative emotions.

CHAPTER SUMMARY

Families find it hard to talk about relations with cognitive impairment and quarrel about putting the person in a care facility. They are also concerns about the cost and quality of care received at such facilities.

IT TAKES A VILLAGE

Extended-care facilities need to realize that the patients need things to help them have roots as they are in a new environment with no memories. De Hogeweyk facilities in Weesp, Netherlands realized this. It has one way in and out and consists of beautiful flowers and fountain. It has facilities like theaters, saloons etc, just like a college would have but it is designed to take care of people with dementia and make them feel like humans and not patients. It focuses on what the patients can do instead of what they can't. Wandering is very common among dementia patients so security is efficient with the help or people, cameras and motion sensors. Every staff is a medical personnel trained to help the patients in their time of need. This is an example of an ideal care facility and as you can see it takes more than just a person to care make it work and care for the patients. One thing to know is to try not to correct a person with dementia, patience is needed. In the early stages, you can challenge them with questions that could help them figure out their reality but never correct them. If this model is adopted in the world, dementia patients would live a fulfilled life till their death.

BRACE YOURSELF

Most people with dementia live at home and caregivers are mostly family members or spouses. It is important to note that when taking care of dementia patients, you should brace yourself for the difficulties and ensure that you take care of yourself as most people end up very stressed. Ask for help from other family members if possible and seek help because doing this takes a huge toll on a person's mental, emotional and physical health as well as their finances. Women are usually the caregivers for people with Alzheimer's and they are usually more likely to develop the disease too. For a long time it was thought that women often got Alzheimer's more than men because they lived longer but research shows it is due to different biology and the process of diagnosis.

There aren't many treatment plans and there is usually lack of consistency and support from the ones available. Not every care facility has the ideal work model to care for patients leaving most of the work to family members. Taking care of a person with advanced dementia tends to be one the reasons families get destabilized financially and emotionally. Taking care of a dementia patient affects different people in different ways and you should try to find the best process that works for you and helps the patient the most.

These are a few things to do after getting a diagnosis for a loved one;

1. Find educative and support programs around you to help increase your knowledge, support you and prepare you for the journey ahead.
2. Find early-stage engagement programs. They help people in early stages of the disease stay active and connected. A dementia patient doesn't have to be confined especially in the early stages.
3. Find clinical trials that could help you and possibly slow the rate at which the disease progresses. There is no guarantee that all will be helpful but it could help gain more knowledge.
4. Keep the home safe: In the early stages, patients could continue regular activities but eventually they would need help doing a lot of tasks. The home also needs to be made safe to prevent accidents and wandering. If the home is not safe, a care facility would be the best option.
5. Make legal plans by taking inventories of legal documents. If these do not exist, an attorney can help make one to help make certain decisions such as making of health decisions, running of the business etc.
6. Make a financial plan to help with possible treatment and drugs, basic needs, care etc. It is better to have a financial adviser to help make these plans and budget. You can also talk to people who have experienced such to help you plan for the obstacles ahead.

7. Build a care team as this is not something that should be done alone. Talk to family, friends, colleagues, medical personnel to help you every step of the way reducing your stress and burden.

KEEP TALKING

Sometimes families find it hard to make decisions and agree on the steps to take when dealing with a patient. When making plans and trying to figure out the best step, ensure you communicate with the other people around you to seek for advice and avoid confusion. Some states use conservatorship when family members cannot agree on a decision. These conservators are guardians and getting this costs more money and could lead to more issues. Conservators have the final say in health, financial and other decisions without needing the opinion of others. Once a conservator is attached, it can be very difficult to remove them. The proceedings tend to be mentally, emotionally and financially draining especially for family members. The best way to avoid the stress of the conservatorship is open communication with family members frequently to make plans and move forward. Plan a meeting physically or virtually to ensure communication with others.

THE INVISIBLE SECOND PATIENT

Caregivers of dementia patients are 6 times more likely to develop dementia than normal people. If you care for a dementia patient, there is a higher risk of it happening to you. This is why the caregivers are the invisible second patients. This situation seems unfair as they already go through the physical, emotional and financial stress. The emotional stress sometimes creates a sense of helplessness for the caregiver. The stress of caregiving could sometimes translate to depression, drug addiction and heart issues. Most people tend to focus on the forgetful part of dementia forgetting there are other symptoms involved that are sometimes very hard to manage. These symptoms are the reasons most patients end up in care facilities as family members cannot keep up or deal with them adequately. Caregivers often feel like they have to be careful around patients to prevent triggering aggressive behaviors and they tend to get worse overtime. In the early stages of dementia, the patient has awareness of their reality, anger, depression etc. 20% of people with Alzheimer's tend to experience increased anxiety, depression, agitation etc, and this is known as Sundowning Syndrome. Later on there are changes in mood, paranoia, delusions etc. and there are no effective treatments for these symptoms.

DON'T FORGET YOURSELF: A NOTE FOR CAREGIVERS

Taking care of a loved one with dementia is usually a team effort but there is always a primary caregiver who does more caregiving. It is important that as a caregiver you prioritize yourself too. This means eat well, engaging in activities and exercises, socialize, take breaks from caregiving etc. If you have a fulltime job while caregiving, ensure you are cautious with your time, needs and emotions or you could breakdown in the long run. Caregiving burnout is caused by the painstaking responsibility the caregiving entails especially when you do not take care of yourself and your needs. If you notice any symptoms of a possible burnout, listen and take a break as the job of caregiving is not an easy one.

Ask for help when needed, talk to people to relieve your emotional burdens. Caregiving is an important responsibility that comes from a place of love and obligation but do not feel bad about taking time for yourself. It helps to identify your motivation in your low times to enable you keep pushing. The hardest obstacle for a caregiver is denial; accepting that a family member has cognitive impairment. There is no preparation for the emotional turmoil this news brings even for someone with medical training. It is not a crime to face denial for awhile. Denial can be a healthy coping mechanism but you cannot exist in that state forever as decisions need to be made. If it is hard to accept the diagnosis, seek professional help.

A lot of caregivers also experience guilt, blaming themselves for not seeing the signs earlier on. Guilt is very common with denial. It is important to be in tune with your emotions, mental health and physical state. Meet similar people for help and advice. Build a support network, keep planning for the future and change your plans if needed. Be mindful of your emotions and needs, do not neglect them. Remember that different patients react differently to a disease; do not think you have it worse than others. Pat yourself for being able to handle the issue and come this far. In the later stages of dementia, repetition is a very common symptom. The patient tends to repeat sentences or activities and the best way to deal with this issue is to stay calm and patient. Engage the patient in a new activity to break the cycle. Share your experience with others, it could help others in need and help people give you more suggestion. The main aim of a caregiver is to help their patient live a good life.

QUESTIONS / EXERCISE

What motivates you to keep going as a caregiver?

_____
_____
_____
_____
_____
_____
_____
_____
_____

How has the illness of a loved one affected you in the past?

_____
_____
_____
_____
_____
_____
_____

What do you do to relieve stress as a caregiver?

_____
_____
_____
_____
_____
_____

Made in United States
Orlando, FL
14 February 2024

43686477R00072